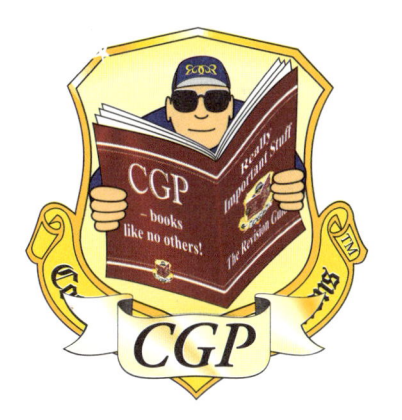

Key Stage Three

Shakespeare

Richard III

This book is for 11-14 year olds.

It's packed with all the really important stuff you need to know about *Richard III* if you want to do well in your Key Stage Three SAT Shakespeare Question.

We've stuck loads of pictures and jokes in to make it more fun — so you'll actually use it.

Simple as that.

What CGP is all about

Our sole aim here at CGP is to produce the highest quality books — carefully written, immaculately presented and dangerously close to being funny.

Then we work our socks off to get them out to you — at the cheapest possible prices.

William Shakespeare (writer, 1564-1616)
Richard III
Here's the background. The two sides of the Royal Family have been at war. Our villainous hero Richard has killed the old King, Henry VI, and his son. Richard's side of the Royal Family now have the Crown. Richard's older brother, Edward IV, is King.
ACT 1
I quite fancy being King. My brother, King Edward IV, is ill — he'll die soon. So I've just got to get rid of my other brother Clarence, and Edward IV's kids, and the throne will be mine. For starters, I'm going to trick Edward IV into getting Clarence killed. Boy, I'm evil...
Richard (our villainous hero)
Act 1 Scene 1
King Edward IV's having me locked up. What's going on?
Clarence (Richard's older brother)
Don't worry bro, I'll sort it out. You know who's to blame for this, don't you? Edward IV's wife Elizabeth and her awful family.
You killed my husband and his dad, you horrid little man.
Yeah, but only cos you're so beautiful. Fancy marrying me?
Ooh you smooth talker. Go on then.
Lady Anne (widow of Henry VI's son)
Act 1 Scene 2
Richard clashes with Queen Elizabeth and her family...
Elizabeth, your family's been spreading lies to turn the King against me.
Rubbish. You're just jealous cos my family's powerful now my husband's King.
None of these vile people deserve any power.
Stanley
Hastings
Buckingham (Richard's buddy)
Queen Elizabeth (Edward IV's wife)
Rivers (Elizabeth's brother)
Grey (Elizabeth's son by a previous marriage)
Margaret (Henry VI's widow — she used to be Queen)
Act 1 Scene 3
A curse on you all! I hope you all die horribly!
Margaret's Curse
Come on, don't kill me, pleeeeease... Ugh.
STAB
1st Murderer
2nd Murderer
Act 1 Scene 4
ACT 2
Clarence is dead, just like you wanted....
What? I changed my mind. I said DON'T kill him after all. Ooh I'm so angry.
King Edward IV (Richard's oldest brother. He's ill and will die soon)
Act 2 Scene 1
Bad news — my husband, Edward IV, has died.
Never mind sis, your son, little Prince Edward can be King now.
Now's my chance to grab the throne. The only thing in my way is Queen Elizabeth and her pesky children....
Let's get 'em.
Act 2 Scene 2
Richard's arrested your relatives, Rivers and Grey.
Messenger
Uh-oh, sounds like my family's in trouble. I wonder if the Princes are OK...
Act 2 Scene 4
The young Princes are brought to Richard...
ACT 3
Welcome to London, kiddies. How d'you fancy a fun holiday locked up in the Tower?
Prince Edward (older son of Edward IV and Queen Elizabeth — heir to the throne)
Duke of York (Prince Edward's little brother)
Act 3 Scene 1
I want to be King so badly. I'll make you an Earl if you support me, Buckingham. As for Hastings, if he's not loyal to me, I'll chop his head off.
Cool.
Stanley realises Richard is up to no good and tries to warn Hastings...
Hastings, I've got a warning from Stanley for you: "Richard's got it in for you. Escape while you can."
Messenger
Rubbish, Richard thinks I'm great.
Hastings
Act 3 Scene 2

Queen Elizabeth's relatives are killed...
Time for the chop lads.
Uh-oh... Margaret's curse has come true.
Let's hope it's not just us who die horribly.
Ratcliffe
Act 3 Scene 3
Hastings is a traitor. Off with his head..
D'oh, if only I'd listened to Stanley's warning...
Act 3 Scene 4
Buckingham, you go and tell everyone the young Princes are illegitimate so that I can become King instead.
Oh Richard, you're so brilliant.
Act 3 Scene 5
Will you be King?
No I couldn't possibly...
Oh go on.
Oh well, if you insist...
Mayor of London
Act 3 Scene 7
ACT 4
We've come to see the Princes.
Well you can't.
I bet Richard is behind this.
I should never have agreed to marry him.
Brackenbury
Anne
Act 4 Scene 1
Soon after Richard and Anne's wedding...
Next we kill the Princes. What do you reckon, Bucks?
Er, that's a bit extreme, isn't it?
And while I'm at it, I'll kill my wife Anne. Boy I'm evil. Ha ha ha..
Act 4 Scene 2
How about that reward you promised me?
Don't hold your breath.
Hmm... I'm going to get out before he decides to kill me. I've heard there's a young guy called Richmond who wants to take the Crown. I'll go and join him...
The Princes are dead.
Good-o.
Tyrrel
Bad news — a young guy called Richmond is raising an army against you. And Buckingham's run off to join him.
Grrrr... Capture them both. Kill them both.
Act 4 Scene 3
We got Buckingham, but Richmond's raised an army and is ready to fight.
Fine. I'll fight him. Get my army!
Catesby
Act 4 Scene 4
ACT 5
The night before battle, Richmond and Richard have the same dream...
Richard's killed all of us... now it's time for him to die... We all hope Richmond wins....
Cripes, that was a scary dream.
Oh, what a nice dream.
Richmond (A young guy who wants to be King)
Act 5 Scene 3
The battle
"A horse! A horse! My kingdom for a horse!" Where's Richmond? I wanna kill him...
Act 5 Scene 4
SPLAT
SLASSSSSH
CRUNCH
And finally, Richard is killed...
Now I want everyone in England to live in peace. And no murdering people this time.
Richmond
Act 5 Scene 5
THE END

Contents

SECTION 1 — THE LOWDOWN ON EXAMS

Preparing Your Answer 1
Writing Well and Giving Examples 2

SECTION 2 — UNDERSTANDING THE PLAY

Stage Directions, Acts and Scenes 3
Richard III as a Play 4
Odd Language 5
More Odd Language 6
Poetry 7
Revision Summary 8

SECTION 3 — THE CHARACTERS

Who's Who in the Play 9
Richard 10
Edward IV, Queen Elizabeth & The Young Princes 11
Lady Anne, Queen Margaret & The Duchess of York 12
The Woodvilles and Clarence 13
The Nobles 14
Richmond and Stanley 15
The Less Important People 16
Revision Summary 17

SECTION 4 — UNDERSTANDING THE STORY

History 18
Fate, Dreams and Omens 19
Crimes, Guilt and Remorse 20
What Happens in Act One (Scenes 1 & 2) 21
What Happens in Act One (Scenes 3 & 4) 22
What Happens in Act Two (Scenes 1-4) 23
What Happens in Act Three (Scenes 1-3) 24
What Happens in Act Three (Scenes 4-7) 25
What Happens in Act Four (Scenes 1-3) 26
What Happens in Act Four (Scenes 4 & 5) 27
What Happens in Act Five (Scenes 1-3) 28
What Happens in Act Five (Scenes 4 & 5) 29
Revision Summary 30

Section 5 — Writing an Essay

Three Steps for an Essay 31
Using Quotes 32
Planning and Structure 33
Writing Your Answer 35
Concluding and Checking for Errors 36
Revision Summary 37

Section 6 — Types of Question

Questions About a Character 38
Characters — The Bigger Picture 39
How Language is Used 40
How Language Creates Mood 41
Writing About a Theme 42
Themes You Might be Asked About 43
Directing a Scene 44
How the Characters Should Speak 45
How the Characters Should Act 46
Appearance & Stage Effects 47
Revision Summary 48

Section 7 — The Set Scenes

Act 1 Scene 2 49
Act 4 Scene 4 53

Index 57

Published by Coordination Group Publications Ltd.

Contributors:
Harriet Knowles
Tim Major
Katherine Reed
Edward Robinson
Elisabeth Sanderson
Gerry Spatharis
Jennifer Underwood
Nicola Woodfin

With thanks to Paula Barnett, Nicola Woodfin and Keri Barrow for the proofreading.

ISBN: 978 1 84762 020 0

Groovy website: www.cgpbooks.co.uk
Jolly bits of clipart from CorelDRAW®
Printed by Elanders Hindson Ltd. Newcastle upon Tyne.

Text, design, layout and original illustrations © Coordination Group Publications Ltd. 2007
All rights reserved.

SECTION 1 — THE LOWDOWN ON EXAMS

Preparing Your Answer

Preparation is the key to doing well in your exam. So, before you start writing, plan what you're going to write. This will make everything a lot easier, even if it sounds like loads of extra work.

You Have to Know the Set Scenes Really Well

1) The Shakespeare paper tests how well you know the play.
2) It's all about the set scenes. Your teacher will tell you which the set scenes are — if you ask them nicely...
3) You have to know these scenes like the back of your hand.

Learn your set scenes... or the puppy gets it.

You'll know which bits of the play you have to write about before the exam — which means you won't get any nasty surprises on the day. As long as you've learnt 'em, that is.

Take Time to Plan Your Answers

Planning might seem like a waste of precious exam time. But if you just start writing without planning you'll end up spouting rubbish. Planning makes your answer loads better.

1) Read the question. Check it out carefully. It could be two questions squished into one:

> **e.g.** Q. In Act 1, Scene 2, what is Anne's opinion of Richard and how does Richard try to change this opinion?

What is Anne's opinion of Richard? ⟵ ⟶ How does Richard try to change this opinion?

2) Read through the scenes again. Look for anything the characters say that will help you answer the question. When you find something useful, underline it. E.g. For the first part of the question above you would look for anything that Anne says about Richard.

3) Next, think about what the main points of your essay will be. Make a list.

> **e.g.**
> - what Anne thinks about Richard
> - the reasons she feels like this
> - how Richard tries to win his way into Anne's affections
> - Anne's initial response to Richard's attempts to win her over
> - how she feels about him by the end of the scene

Do you see my point?

4) Include all your main points in the essay. Then you'll be on your way to a good mark.

Preparation, that's what you need...

You'll feel a lot more relaxed once you've got a good plan to fall back on. Once that's sorted you can focus on each point one at a time. This makes the whole exam thing a lot less scary.

Writing Well and Giving Examples

Examiners are a funny lot, but it's easy enough to impress them if you know what makes them tick. Here's a few useful little tricks that'll have them gasping in admiration.

Use Examples to Show You Know Your Stuff

It's crucial that you use examples. They show evidence of the points you're making. As my old granny used to say, "An opinion without an example is like a boy-band without a rubbish dance routine." Or something.

Quotes are really useful examples. Examiners love 'em. Remember to:

1) Start and end quotes with speech marks.
2) Copy out the words exactly as they are in the play.
3) Explain why the quote is a good example — what does it tell you?

I couldn't unlock the key scenes.

Sort Out Your Writing

1) Sound enthusiastic about the play. Use plenty of adjectives (descriptive words).

   e.g. *The atmosphere in this scene is very tense and menacing — Shakespeare shows the audience that Richard is an evil character who will stop at nothing in order to become King.*

2) Check your spelling and punctuation. Otherwise the examiner might not know what you mean.
3) Write in paragraphs. A page that's full of writing with no breaks is tough to read. Remember, a new topic = a new paragraph.

Write About Versions of the Play You've Seen

If you've seen a film or theatre version of the play, you can write about that too — as long as it relates to the question.

This is another good way of sounding interested in the play. Just make sure you mention which version of the play you saw.

Keep in mind that each version can be very different. The costumes, settings and personalities of the characters can all vary.

e.g. *In the production of the play I saw in Barnsley in 2002, the director, Ivor Megaphone, brought out the sense of danger in this scene by reducing the lighting and making Richard talk in a quiet, calculating way.*

I'll make an exam-ple of you...

Exams aren't really that complicated. They ask you a question, you answer it. If you're prepared, there'll be no nasty surprises. Stick to the point, and there's nowt to worry about.

Section 1 — The Lowdown on Exams

Section 2 — Understanding the Play

Stage Directions, Acts and Scenes

It's really important you know what stage directions, acts and scenes are. Acts and scenes are like the skeleton of the play, and stage directions tell you what's going on on-stage.

Stage Directions Tell You Who's Doing What

Stage directions tell the actors what to do, e.g. when to come on stage and when to go off. They sometimes say who they have to talk to as well. They're usually written in italics or put in brackets:

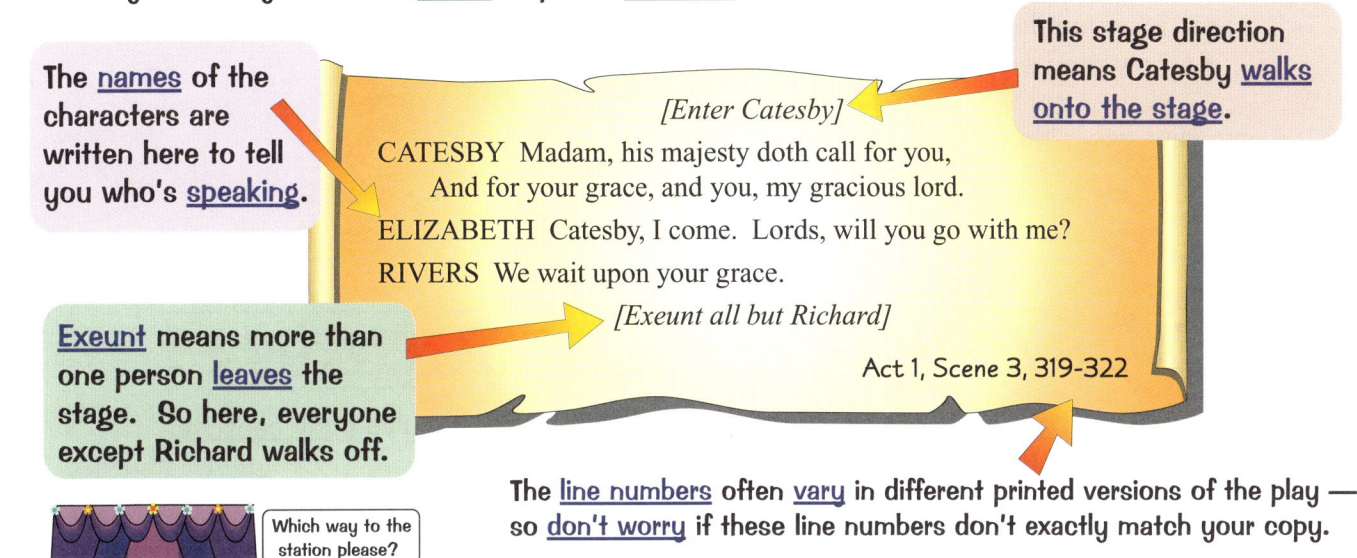

The names of the characters are written here to tell you who's speaking.

This stage direction means Catesby walks onto the stage.

[Enter Catesby]
CATESBY Madam, his majesty doth call for you,
 And for your grace, and you, my gracious lord.
ELIZABETH Catesby, I come. Lords, will you go with me?
RIVERS We wait upon your grace.
[Exeunt all but Richard]

Act 1, Scene 3, 319-322

Exeunt means more than one person leaves the stage. So here, everyone except Richard walks off.

Which way to the station please?

The line numbers often vary in different printed versions of the play — so don't worry if these line numbers don't exactly match your copy.

Remember, plays are supposed to be performed, not read. So stage directions are really helpful for imagining how the play would look on-stage.

Acts and Scenes Split Up the Play

1) The play is divided up into five big chunks called acts. Each act tells us part of the story. Put them all together and you get the whole story.

2) Acts are also divided up into even smaller chunks called scenes. Scenes break up the story. A new scene might be in a different place, at a different time, or with different characters.

 E.g. If one scene is set in the Tower, the next scene could be outside, in a street. Or one scene might be set during the day, and the next at night.

Are you sure this is the right scene?

Stop it, you're making a scene...

Acts and scenes are actually really handy, as they can help you find the speech or bit of action you're looking for. Remember — the play has 5 acts and loads of scenes.

Section 2 — Understanding the Play

Richard III as a Play

Check out these tips and you'll really get to grips with the play.

It's a Play, Not a Novel

It's meant to be acted, not just read. When you read the play, it's hard to imagine what it will look like on stage. Try and see the characters in your mind. Think about:

- what kind of people they are
- how you think they would say their lines
- how they would act

Oi, Shakespeare, how's the new book going?
Whatever.
It's a play, actually.

If you want some idea of how the play might look when it's acted out, you could watch it on video or DVD. Your school might have a copy of it — it's worth asking. Just remember: each version will be different.

Sometimes Characters Talk to Themselves

1) In real life, this is odd. In plays, it's normal — it doesn't mean they've gone bananas.

[Aside] That zebra's gonna make a tasty lunch.
It's so lovely and peaceful today...

2) The characters talk to themselves to let the audience know what they are thinking and how they are feeling.

3) When someone talks to themself on an empty stage, it's called a soliloquy (or monologue).

4) If someone talks to the audience when there are other people on stage, it'll say [Aside] by their name in the play. The audience can hear what is being said, but the other characters can't.

Richard III is a History Play

Shakespeare wrote a series of plays about the history of the English Royal Family. Richard III follows on from Henry VI Part 3, and it's set about 80 years before Shakespeare was born.

Even though it's a history play, that doesn't mean it's pure fact. Shakespeare chose to base the play on the idea that Richard was a deformed murderer and Richmond was a good man — but this is only one of several versions of events. Shakespeare even made up some characters and changed some of the dates to make the play more entertaining for his audience.

Richard III is also sometimes called a tragedy, as the main character rises to power before losing and being killed, and there are loads of deaths.

Richard the Furred — Shakespeare acted by cats...

If you're not used to reading plays, it's bound to feel odd at first. The fact that the play was written ages ago, combined with the main characters being royals and nobles, takes some getting used to.

Section 2 — Understanding the Play

Odd Language

Some of this old language is hard to get your head round. But once you get the hang of reading it things will become a lot clearer. Just remember these rules:

Don't Stop Reading at the End of a Line

1) Follow the punctuation — read to the end of the sentence, not the end of the line.

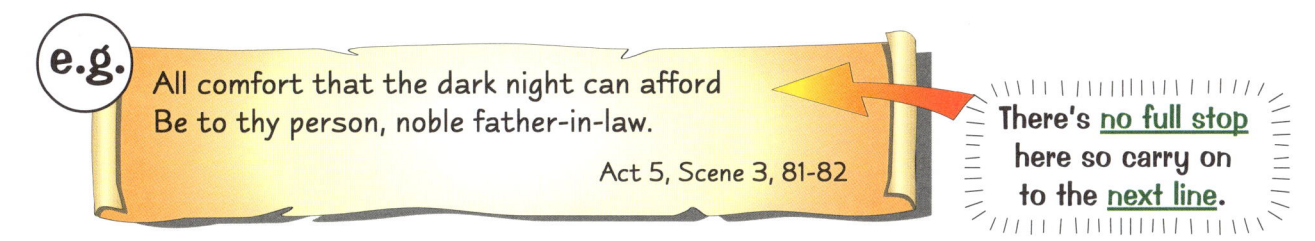

> e.g.
> All comfort that the dark night can afford
> Be to thy person, noble father-in-law.
> *Act 5, Scene 3, 81-82*

There's no full stop here so carry on to the next line.

2) These two lines actually make up one sentence:

> All comfort that the dark night can afford be to thy person, noble father-in-law.

3) Most lines start with a capital letter — but this doesn't always mean it's a new sentence.

4) Full stops, question marks and exclamation marks show you where the sentence ends.

Sometimes You Have to Switch the Words Around

1) Shakespeare likes to mess around with the order of words. It helps him fit the sentences into the poetry (see page 7).

2) If a piece of writing looks like it's back-to-front — don't panic.

> e.g.
> Here in these confines slily have I lurked
> *Act 4, Scene 4, line 3*

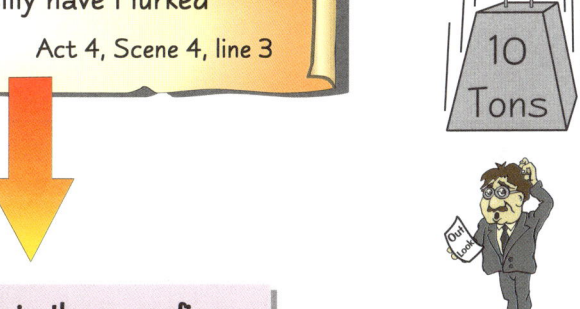

3) Play around with the word order and it'll make sense. What this really says is:

> I have slily lurked here in these confines.

Sense make doesn't Shakespeare...

I know Shakespeare's language looks really different from the English we speak, but it's actually pretty similar. Once you've got the word order sorted you're well on the way to sussing it out.

Section 2 — Understanding the Play

More Odd Language

Shakespeare was around over 400 years ago — so the language he uses can seem a bit weird. Some of the words are old words that we don't use any more.

Thou, Thee and Thy Come Up a Lot

Once you know what these words mean, things get a lot easier. Happy days.

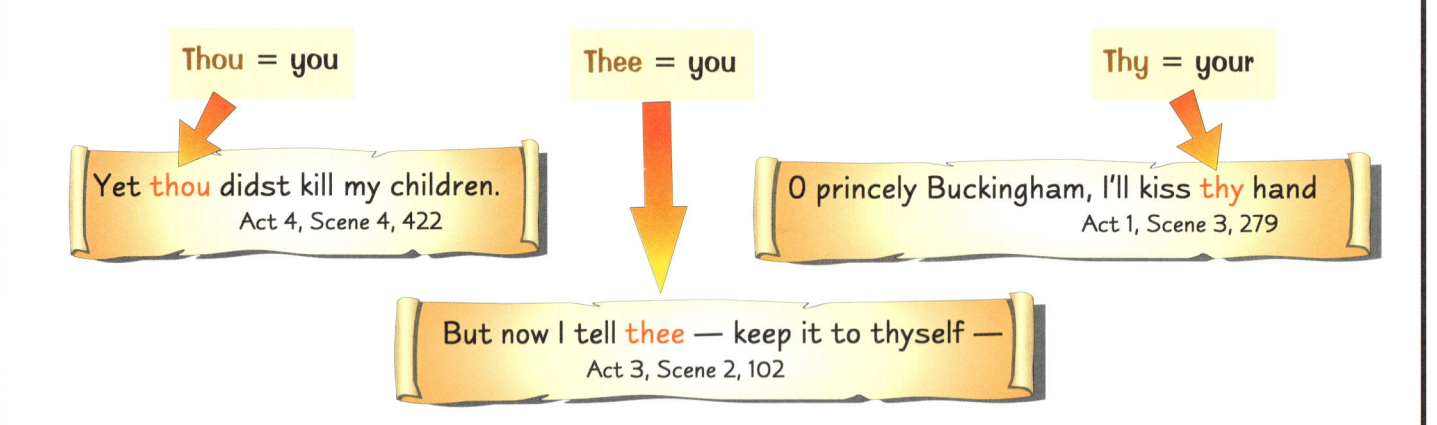

Thou = you

Yet thou didst kill my children.
Act 4, Scene 4, 422

Thee = you

But now I tell thee — keep it to thyself —
Act 3, Scene 2, 102

Thy = your

O princely Buckingham, I'll kiss thy hand
Act 1, Scene 3, 279

Verbs Can Look Odd

Hast thou seen the size of this carrot?

Often, all that's different is there's a couple of extra letters on the end of the verb. Take off the t or st and you'll see what they mean.

e.g.
- hath, hast = has
- wilt = will
- didst = did
- thinkst = think
- speakst = speak

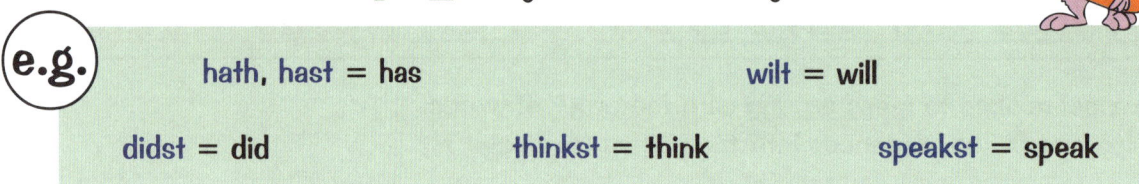

These verbs often go with thou, like this:

If thou wilt outstrip death, go cross the seas
Act 4, Scene 1, 41

Some Words are Squashed Together

The word it often gets stuck to the next word, and loses the "i".

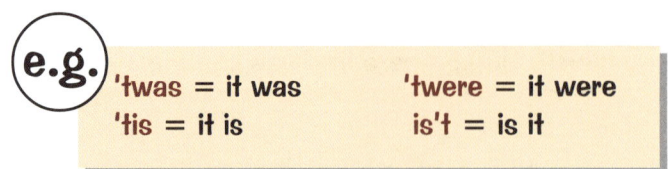

e.g.
- 'twas = it was
- 'twere = it were
- 'tis = it is
- is't = is it

'Tis an outrage!

An i for an i...

Dropping letters from words isn't that strange when you think about it. We still do it in modern English, like when we change it is to it's. Shakespeare just drops different letters.

Section 2 — Understanding the Play

Poetry

There's lots of <u>poetry</u> in Shakespeare's plays. If you understand the poetry, it'll <u>help you understand</u> some of the reasons behind the <u>strange language</u>.

How to Spot Poetry

<u>Prose</u> means writing that <u>isn't poetry</u>.
There's a lot of <u>poetry</u> in Richard III — and <u>here's how to spot it</u>:

> **Poetry has:**
> 1) Capital letters at the start of each line
> 2) 10, 11 or 12 syllables in each line

A <u>syllable</u> is a unit of sound. The word <u>poetry</u> has 3 syllables – <u>po</u> <u>e</u> <u>try</u>.

Poetry Doesn't Have to Rhyme

1) Some poetry <u>rhymes</u>, some <u>doesn't</u>.

e.g.
> I died for hope ere I could lend thee aid.
> But cheer thy heart and be thou not dismayed.
> God and good angels fight on Richmond's side,
> And Richard falls in height of all his pride.
> Act 5, Scene 3, 174-177

Each line starts with a <u>capital letter</u>.

This bit of poetry is in <u>rhyming couplets</u> — the first line rhymes with the second, and the third rhymes with the fourth.

e.g.
> I will converse with iron-witted fools
> And unrespective boys. None are for me
> That look into me with considerate eyes.
> High-reaching Buckingham grows circumspect.
> Act 4, Scene 2, 28-31

This <u>doesn't rhyme</u> — but it's <u>still poetry</u>.

2) The language sometimes sounds <u>strange</u> because Shakespeare tries to get <u>each line</u> to contain the <u>right amount of syllables</u>.

3) Most of Richard III is written in poetry — although some of the <u>less posh</u> characters, like the murderers, sometimes talk in <u>prose</u> (speech that isn't poetry).

You did ask for three silly bulls?

Leann Rimes — with what?

Once you realise you're dealing with <u>poetry</u>, it becomes much easier to work out <u>what it means</u>. And the rules for <u>spotting it</u> are pretty simple — just remember that it doesn't have to rhyme.

Section 2 — Understanding the Play

Revision Summary

Right, let's see how much you know about Bill Shakespeare and his odd little ways. If you haven't read any of Shakespeare's stuff before, it's easy to be flummoxed by the way he writes. But trust me, the more you read, the easier it gets. If you get stuck on any of these questions, look back through the section to find the answers. Then have another go, without looking back.

1) What's the point of stage directions?
2) What does "exeunt" mean?
3) What's the play split up into?
    a) Chapters and verses   b) Nooks and crannies   c) Acts and scenes
4) A play is meant to be:
    a) ignored   b) burnt   c) performed
5) What is a soliloquy?
6) If it says "Aside" by a character's name, who can hear what they're saying?
    a) The other characters   b) The audience   c) Belgians
7) The events in Richard III are:
    a) pure fact   b) just one version of events   c) set in Bulgaria
8) "A new line of poetry means it's a new sentence." True or false?
9) If a piece of writing doesn't make sense, what should you do?
    a) Change the word order   b) Phone a friend   c) Cry
10) When was Shakespeare around?
    a) 400 years ago   b) 200 years ago   c) 65 million years ago
11) What do these words mean?
    a) Thou   b) Hath   c) Didst   d) 'Twas
12) What does each line of poetry start with?
13) How many syllables are there in a line of poetry?
14) Does all poetry rhyme?

Section 2 — Understanding the Play

Section 3 — The Characters

Who's Who in the Play

There are loads of characters in this play. Here are some of the important ones.

Richard III — the main baddie

He's sometimes called the Duke of Gloucester. He's the most important character. He makes things happen — most of them bad.

Buckingham and Richard's supporters

Buckingham gives Richard a lot of help, but then they fall out and Richard has him killed. Richard hires Tyrrel to kill the young Princes. Brakenbury's in charge of the Tower. Catesby and Ratcliffe are more cronies.

Edward IV and Queen Elizabeth

Edward IV is Richard III's brother. Edward IV is King to start with but he soon dies. Queen Elizabeth is his wife.

The Young Princes, sons of Edward IV and Elizabeth

Prince Edward is next in line to the throne after Edward IV dies. Richard has him and his brother, the young Duke of York, killed.

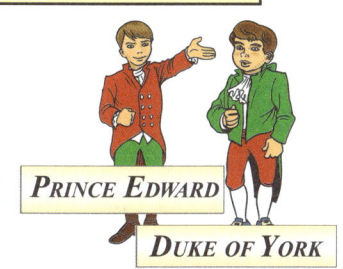

Clarence and Hastings

Clarence is Richard's other brother. Richard has him killed in Act 1. Hastings is a nobleman who is also killed by Richard.

Rivers, Dorset and Grey

These are the Woodvilles. Earl Rivers is Queen Elizabeth's brother. The Marquis of Dorset and Lord Grey are her sons by an earlier marriage. Richard has Rivers and Grey locked up and executed. Dorset gets away.

Queen Margaret, Lady Anne and The Duchess of York

Queen Margaret was married to Henry VI, the old King — until Richard killed him. Lady Anne was married to Margaret's son, until Richard killed him too. Richard marries Lady Anne then has her killed. The Duchess is Richard's mum.

Richmond and Stanley — Richard's opponents

Richmond is Richard's rival for the throne. He fights Richard and kills him. Richmond becomes King Henry VII. Stanley is a nobleman who secretly supports Richmond.

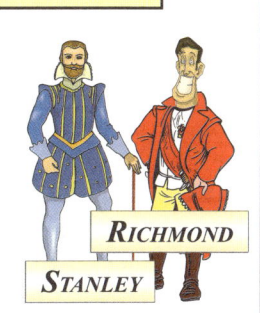

Richard

As you might have guessed from the title, Richard is the most important character in the play.

He's Ambitious and Determined to Succeed

1) He's bold and confident. He tells us right at the start that he's out to cause trouble.

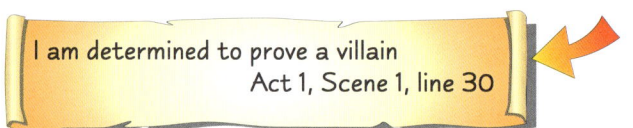

> I am determined to prove a villain
> Act 1, Scene 1, line 30

2) He's a good fighter and brave in battle.

3) He's very ambitious. He'll do anything for power — he's willing to have his own brother and his young nephews killed so that he can become King.

He's Bad Through and Through

1) Richard says he's so ugly that the dogs bark at him. He's "deformed" and lame. Some of the other characters comment on his bad looks too.

2) In Shakespeare's time, an audience would expect a character who looked bad to behave badly — and Richard doesn't disappoint them. He chooses to be bad.

3) Several other characters say they're sorry for their bad deeds before they die, but Richard doesn't.

> Conscience is but a word that cowards use
> Act 5, Scene 3, line 310

4) He only cares about himself. He's two-faced and unreliable — even to the people who help him. He uses people then gets rid of them.

He's Crafty and Clever — and a Great Actor

1) Richard can be witty and charming as well as sarcastic. He flatters people and fools them with his clever words. He sets out to persuade Lady Anne to marry him — even though he has just killed her husband — and he manages it.

2) He's good at changing the way he speaks to play different parts. When he woos Lady Anne he pretends to be romantic. He acts the sympathetic brother with Clarence and he's humble and religious in front of the Mayor and citizens. It's all just an act.

You should hear my Johnny Vegas impression. Monkey!

3) He tells loads of lies, e.g. he spreads rumours about the young Princes being illegitimate so that he can be King. He promises Buckingham rewards for his help, but never delivers them.

You know I'm bad, I'm bad, I'm really really bad...

Richard is an out-and-out villain — we have absolutely no sympathy whatsoever when he cops it. But at the same time, you can't help admiring his cleverness and determination. Ooh, he's a devil...

Section 3 — The Characters

Edward IV, Queen Elizabeth & The Young Princes

King Edward IV is <u>married</u> to Queen Elizabeth. They have two young <u>sons</u> — Edward, Prince of Wales and Richard, Duke of York. They have a <u>daughter</u> too, called Elizabeth, but she doesn't appear.

Edward IV Tries but Fails to Keep Peace

1) At the start, Edward IV is <u>King</u>. He's <u>ill</u> and dies early in the play.

2) Edward IV's <u>suspicious</u> of his brother Clarence. Richard persuades Edward to have <u>Clarence killed</u>. Edward <u>changes his mind</u> afterwards but can't save Clarence. He feels really guilty about Clarence's death.

3) Edward seems to be a decent King but his <u>judgement</u> is <u>poor</u>. He made a <u>big mistake</u> in trusting Richard.

4) Edward tries to make sure everyone has sorted out their <u>quarrels</u> before he dies. He insists they all make up and swear to be <u>friends</u>. He wants to die with a <u>clear conscience</u>.

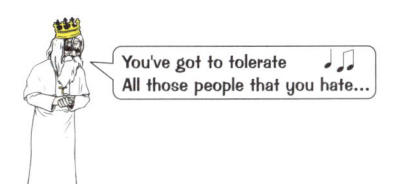

You've got to tolerate All those people that you hate...

> And more in peace my soul shall part to heaven,
> Since I have made my friends at peace on earth
> Act 2, Scene 1, 5-6

Queen Elizabeth Survives

1) Queen Elizabeth's genuinely <u>upset</u> when her husband, Edward IV, dies. She says she could cry enough to "drown the world". After Edward's death, her brother, Rivers, and one of her sons, Grey, are <u>executed</u>. Later on her two <u>youngest sons</u> are killed by Richard.

2) Queen Elizabeth learns to <u>stand up for herself</u> as the play goes on. At first she's <u>not very strong</u> — she rushes off into <u>sanctuary</u> (safety in church) when Richard arrests Rivers and Grey. But by the end of the play she <u>stands up to Richard</u>. She <u>interrupts</u> him and <u>argues</u> when he asks to marry her daughter.

3) She's clever enough to <u>protect her daughter</u>, also called Elizabeth, from Richard and then arrange for her to <u>marry Richmond</u> instead.

The Young Princes are Innocent Victims

1) Prince Edward and his brother the Duke of York are only <u>children</u>, but they're next in line to the <u>throne</u> after Edward IV dies. They behave so well that it's <u>shocking</u> when they die. Even their murderer <u>Tyrrel</u> (see p.16) feels bad about them being killed.

But we're so cute...

2) Prince Edward is <u>brave</u> and <u>obedient</u> — even though he's anxious about staying in the Tower. He wants to <u>serve his country</u> well.

3) The Duke of York is <u>witty</u> and <u>lively</u>. He's almost as good at <u>word play</u> as his Uncle Richard.

Get out, before I have you throne out...

Richard plays his brother Edward IV like a trumpet — he gets him to do exactly what Richard wants. Elizabeth starts off a bit rubbish but in the end she double-crosses Richard, so fair play to her.

Section 3 — The Characters

Lady Anne, Queen Margaret & The Duchess of York

These three women are quite different from each other — but they all hate Richard.

Lady Anne is Another of Richard's Victims

1) She was married to the old Prince Edward, but Richard killed him and his father, Henry VI. She curses Richard pretty viciously — she even calls him a "foul lump of deformity" — but Richard still persuades her to marry him.

2) Lady Anne's quite weak and lonely. She doesn't want to be Queen and she seems unhappy all the time.

3) She is kind to Clarence's children and tries to visit the young Princes in the Tower. The Young Duke of York is very fond of her. The Duchess of York likes her too.

4) Richard gets rid of Anne very quickly after marrying her, because he decides he wants to marry Queen Elizabeth's daughter. He starts a rumour that Anne's ill. The next thing we hear is that she's dead.

Well, no one's perfect. At least Richard's got prospects...

Queen Margaret Curses Everyone

1) She's bitter and angry right from the start of the play. Her husband, Henry VI, and son were killed by Richard. She thinks she should still be Queen and she wants revenge for her dead husband and son.

2) She's ferocious and good with words. Some of her curses are great. She calls Richard a "bottled spider" and she stands up to him even when he makes fun of her.

3) The others laugh at Margaret at first. She predicts that they'll be sorry and she's right. She even warns Buckingham against Richard but he ignores her.

4) Later on, she gloats at all the destruction Richard has caused. She thinks it serves them all right.

The Duchess of York Hates her Son Richard

1) The Duchess of York's ashamed of Richard and says he was a horrible child. She wishes she'd strangled him at birth. That might seem a bit rough coming from your own mother. Richard doesn't care though. He's just sarcastic and rude to her.

2) She's very upset when her sons Clarence and Edward IV die. We can see she loves her grandsons (the young Princes) but they're killed too. No wonder the Duchess curses Richard — just like Lady Anne and Queen Margaret do.

3) By the end of the play the Duchess has had enough. She says she's seen too much trouble and she just wants to die.

Now then, shall I marry the hideous murderer or not..?

If you find yourself shouting "NOOOOO! DON'T MARRY HIM, YOU MUPPET!" at Lady Anne when Richard chats her up, you're not the only one. It's hard to understand why Anne agrees to it.

Section 3 — The Characters

The Woodvilles and Clarence

The Woodvilles — Rivers, Grey and Dorset — are Queen Elizabeth's relatives.
The Duke of Clarence is Richard's brother (he's older than Richard but younger than Edward IV).

The Woodvilles Have a Hard Time of it

1) Richard doesn't like the Woodvilles. He's annoyed that they've become powerful now that Elizabeth is Queen.

2) Earl Rivers looks after his sister, Queen Elizabeth. He offers her good advice, e.g. it's his idea to get young Prince Edward crowned as soon as possible after King Edward IV's death. Rivers is suspicious of Richard — just like Elizabeth is.

> Let him be crowned. In him your comfort lives.
> Drown desperate sorrow in dead Edward's grave
> And plant your joys in living Edward's throne.
> Act 2, Scene 2, 98-100

3) The Woodvilles know their duty. Edward IV tells them to make up with their enemies, Hastings and Buckingham, so they do. They're loyal to young Prince Edward as well.

4) Rivers and Grey are imprisoned and killed at Pomfret Castle on Richard's orders. Their friend Sir Thomas Vaughan is executed with them. All three appear to Richard and Richmond as ghosts at the end of the play.

5) Queen Elizabeth's other son, the Marquis of Dorset, gets away. Elizabeth tells Dorset to go abroad and join Richmond. It's a good plan — Richmond wins and Dorset survives.

Clarence Feels Guilty About his Past

1) Clarence has got a dodgy past — he plotted against his brother Edward IV during the Wars of the Roses. Later on he changed back to Edward's side. He feels bad about it though. He says sorry for his treason before he dies.

> I'm not a pheasant plucker
> I'm a pheasant plucker's mate
> And I'm only plucking pheasants
> Cos the pheasant plucker's late.

2) Clarence is good with words. He has a horrible nightmare about drowning and he describes it in vivid detail. He talks one of the murderers out of killing him, but then the other one kills him.

3) He's fooled by Richard's fake sympathy. He doesn't find out Richard has tricked him until the very last minute. It's too late by then of course.

4) Clarence cares deeply about his family. He pleads for them not to be punished for his mistakes.

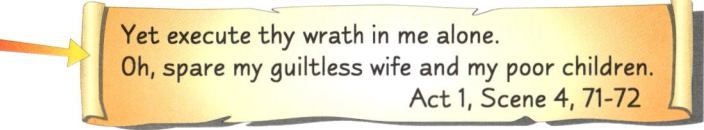

> Yet execute thy wrath in me alone.
> Oh, spare my guiltless wife and my poor children.
> Act 1, Scene 4, 71-72

5) He has a horrible death. He's stabbed then drowned in a barrel of wine.

Grey's a colourful character...

So that's another four victims of Richard then: Rivers, Grey, Vaughan and Clarence. At least Dorset gets away in time. There's a lot to be said for taking good advice when someone offers it.

Section 3 — The Characters

The Nobles

This lot are a bunch of Lords and Dukes who have to choose whether to be on Richard's side or not. It's pretty dangerous either way.

Buckingham is Richard's Sidekick

1) The Duke of Buckingham does a lot to help Richard become King. Buckingham's cunning and happy to lie and trick people. He pretends he has to persuade Richard to accept the position of King and does a stirring speech about what a brilliant ruler Richard will be.

Honestly, Richard's lovely. You just don't know him like I do.

2) Buckingham is ambitious and he trusts Richard to reward him for his help. Richard flatters him and calls him "my other self". Buckingham gets a little too pleased with himself.

3) Buckingham has his limits. He's not sure about the plan to murder the Princes and so Richard turns against him. Buckingham tries to run away but he ends up being executed. We finally see a decent side to Buckingham when he admits that he deserves to die.

Hastings Underestimates Richard — Big Mistake

1) Lord Hastings doesn't understand how dangerous Richard is. He thinks Richard and Buckingham like him and he says Richard is so honest that you can always tell what he's thinking. The audience knows Hastings is wrong.

2) Hastings is loyal to Edward IV and the young Prince Edward, which is why he won't support Richard to be King. You can admire him for that — but it doesn't do him much good.

3) Hastings is very foolish. He ignores a warning from Stanley that he should get away from Richard, and he's shocked when Richard suddenly orders his execution.

Some Others Help Richard Carry Out his Plans

1) William Catesby does a lot of errands. He's as two-faced as Buckingham and helps to get Richard crowned. Catesby stays loyal to Richard right to the end.

2) Sir Richard Ratcliffe and Lord Lovell do the dirty work. They organise a lot of the executions. Ratcliffe's with Richard at the end and tries to comfort him after his nightmare.

3) Sir Robert Brakenbury is the Lieutenant of the Tower. He has to keep an eye on a lot of Richard's prisoners like Clarence and the young princes.

4) Norfolk and Surrey are on Richard's side but Herbert, Oxford and Blunt fight for Richmond.

"Nobles" in name only then...

There are quite a few of these noblemen, and it's easy to get them mixed up. Buckingham's the most important — if Richard's Mr Burns, then Buckingham's his Smithers. Hastings' plight serves as a warning about how dangerous Richard is — if you don't support him, you'd best be careful.

Section 3 — The Characters

Richmond and Stanley

These two are the goodies who bring peace to England at the end of the play.
Stanley is Richmond's stepfather — he's married to Richmond's mum.

Richmond is the Hero — he Kills Richard

1) Henry, Earl of Richmond has a claim to the throne through the Lancastrian side of the Royal Family. He kills Richard III in the Battle of Bosworth at the end of the play and becomes King Henry VII. He puts an end to years of fighting between the Houses of York and Lancaster by bringing the two sides together. He becomes the first Tudor king.

2) Richmond's what a good King should be. He's brave in battle and he gives a good speech to encourage his men. People are loyal to him. The ghosts of Richard's victims all wish him success too.

3) Richmond's quite different from Richard. He's straightforward and he's got a clear conscience. He sleeps well before the battle and is optimistic and confident.

4) People call him "virtuous" and "holy", and he prays to God for success. He wants to win for the sake of peace and justice — not because he's greedy or wants power.

With my winning smile and perfect teeth, I've just got to win. Hurrah!

> In God's name, cheerly on, courageous friends,
> To reap the harvest of perpetual peace
> By this one bloody trial of sharp war.
> Act 5, Scene 2, 14-16

Stanley Secretly Supports Richmond

1) Lord Stanley is also known as the Earl of Derby. He pretends to be on Richard's side, but secretly sends Richmond messages of support. He gives good advice and encouragement to Richmond.

Ooh, aren't I a tease?

2) Stanley tries to warn Hastings to be careful — but Hastings doesn't listen.

3) Stanley's wise and cautious. Even Richard isn't quite sure whose side he's on. He's one of the few who sees through Richard — but he's clever enough not to speak out against him until the time is right.

4) He wants what's best for the country — not just what's best for himself. He chooses to go and support Richmond even though it means leaving his son George in danger. It's a brave thing to do.

Stanley, don't turn to the dark side...

Richmond turns out to be a very important character, although we don't get to meet him until Act 5. Stanley's an interesting bloke who's lurking around throughout the play, although it's not clear exactly where his loyalties lie until fairly near the end.

Section 3 — The Characters

The Less Important People

A lot of these people don't say much but play a part in Richard's plans, sometimes without realising.

Some Characters are Involved in Killing People

1) Tyrrel is proud and greedy. He organises the murders of the two young Princes in the Tower of London, but he says afterwards how terrible it was. The two tough guys he got to do it — Dighton and Forrest — actually cried.

Are you sure you're the right Sheriff?
Darn tootin', pardner.

2) There are some officials like the Sheriff. He takes Buckingham to his execution.

3) The Keeper of the Tower has to guard Clarence. He's respectful to him.

4) There are two murderers who come to kill Clarence as well.

Some Characters Talk About What's Happening

1) Three Citizens (ordinary town people) discuss what's going to happen after King Edward IV's death. One of them thinks things will be fine, but another says Prince Edward is too young to rule, and this might cause trouble.

2) The Scrivener has written out the legal charges against Hastings. He tells us that the charges are false, but no one dares say so.

3) The Lord Mayor is fooled by Richard and Buckingham. They tell him that Hastings has been plotting and he believes it. The Mayor also believes it when Richard pretends to be religious as well, and he pleads with Richard to become King.

4) There's a Pursuivant (a royal messenger) who chats to Hastings, and lots of other servants, messengers and pages.

Richard Uses the Church Officials for his Plans

1) The Bishop of Ely goes scurrying off for strawberries when Richard tells him to. Later on he goes over to Richmond's side.

2) The Lord Cardinal (Archbishop of Canterbury) is persuaded by Buckingham to take the young Duke of York away from his mother to join his brother in the Tower.

3) The Archbishop of York is anxious and confused. He helps Queen Elizabeth run off to safety after they hear that her family have been arrested.

4) Sir Christopher Urswick is a priest who takes a letter of support from Stanley to Richmond.

5) There's also a random priest who greets Hastings on his way to the Tower.

Shakespearean pit workers — the miner characters...

Don't worry if you get these characters a bit confused, e.g. if you forget who the strawberry-specialist is. A lot of them, like the murderers, are named after what they do, which helps.

Section 3 — The Characters

Revision Summary

You need to be confident about who all the characters are and why they're important. There are some pretty complicated relationships in there — once you've sussed out who does what to who, you can get on with writing cracking essays. If you're not clear about this stuff, studying the play will be harder than dragging Dawn French up Mount Snowdon wearing flip-flops. Check you can answer all these questions.

1) How would Shakespeare's audience expect Richard to behave from his appearance?
2) How does Richard act in front of the Mayor?
3) How does Richard let Buckingham down?
    a) He kills Buckingham's brother.
    b) He promises to reward him but doesn't.
    c) He forgets to pick him up from the dentist's.
4) Who's Queen Elizabeth's husband?
5) How does Queen Elizabeth react when Rivers and Grey are arrested?
6) Who's Prince Edward's brother?
7) What happened to Lady Anne's husband?
8) Why does Richard have Lady Anne killed?
9) Why is Queen Margaret so bitter?
10) What does the Duchess of York say Richard was like when he was a child?
11) Who are the Woodvilles?
12) Why does Clarence feel guilty?
13) How does Buckingham help Richard out?
    a) He kills Queen Margaret.
    b) He helps Richard become King.
    c) He gets him tickets for Pop Idol.
14) What happens to Buckingham in the end?
15) What does Hastings reckon Richard and Buckingham think of him?
16) Who's the Lieutenant of the Tower?
17) Who kills Richard at the end?
    a) Richmond
    b) Stanley
    c) Margaret
18) How is Stanley related to Richmond?
19) Who organises the murders of the young Princes?
20) What does the Scrivener think about the charges against Hastings?
21) What part does the Lord Cardinal play in Richard's schemes?

Section 3 — The Characters

SECTION 4 — UNDERSTANDING THE STORY

History

Shakespeare wrote Richard III in 1593, when Queen Elizabeth I was on the throne.

The Play is Based on Real History

1) Shakespeare used a lot of characters who really existed. The royal family was real, and so were the Woodvilles, Buckingham, Stanley and Hastings.

2) The play is set in 1485. The Wars of the Roses had been going on for more than 35 years. These were real battles between different branches of the royal family — the House of York and the House of Lancaster. Each House thought they should be ruling the country.

3) Henry VI was a Lancastrian. After his death, Edward IV, who was a Yorkist, became King. After he died, his brother Richard III (also a Yorkist) became King. He was killed at the Battle of Bosworth, and the Earl of Richmond became King Henry VII.

4) Henry VII was a Lancastrian, but he united the two Houses by marrying a Yorkist. He became the first Tudor King, ending the wars.

Shakespeare Changed Some Events

1) Shakespeare made up some things and changed some characters. He wanted to make his play exciting and dramatic.

Maybe I should add some killer robots... No, don't be silly. I've got it — Buckingham leaves to go and live in Perth...

2) For example, the young Princes really did disappear — but there's no proof Richard killed them.

3) The real Queen Margaret had already died by the time the events in the play happened — she didn't really hang on in there cursing people.

Richard III was Probably Not As Bad in Real Life

1) Shakespeare made Richard III come across as pretty evil. People used to believe that if you were bad inside it would show in an ugly appearance. So Shakespeare made him deformed and horrible to look at and gave him a warped personality.

2) Shakespeare also made Richmond a typical good guy. He's the first Tudor King and he only challenges Richard's rule because he wants to rescue England from chaos.

3) Queen Elizabeth I would have been happy with this version, because Richmond was her grandfather. During her reign, it became popular to exaggerate how evil Richard III was.

This is sometimes called the Tudor Myth.
It basically means:
Henry VII (Richmond) = good,
Richard III = very, very bad.

One false move and you're history...

Don't worry, you don't need to know all the ins and outs of medieval history. But it's useful to know some background, like the Wars of the Roses, as it helps make sense of what happens in the play.

Fate, Dreams and Omens

Richard III is bound to fail because he becomes King by doing wrong. Shakespeare included lots of omens and prophecies to make it seem even more inevitable.

Richard Thinks he's In Control — but he's Wrong

1) The first prophecy we hear about is one that King Edward IV heard. A wizard told him that someone whose name begins with "G" would murder his heirs. Richard uses this to make Edward suspicious of Clarence, whose first name is George. In fact the "G" stands for Gloucester — Richard is the Duke of Gloucester, and it's Richard who kills them.

2) Henry VI said that Richmond would be king. And an Irish prophet told Richard that he wouldn't live long after he saw Richmond. These prophecies hint that Richard can't win — however confident he seems.

3) The ghosts which appear to Richard and Richmond before the battle confirm this. They tell Richard to despair and die and they tell Richmond to expect victory.

A lot of the Curses we hear Come True

1) Lady Anne curses Richard over the coffin of Henry VI. She also curses his future wife — which turns out to be her. Whoops.

2) Queen Margaret curses the other characters so severely that even Buckingham is frightened.

> My hair doth stand on end to hear her curses.
> Act 1, Scene 3, line 303

MARGARET'S CURSES
- She hopes that Edward IV's son, the young Prince Edward, will die young.
- She wants Queen Elizabeth to see her children die.
- She says that Rivers, Dorset and Hastings will die early.
- She wishes Richard bad dreams and friends who turn against him.

Several Characters have Meaningful Dreams

1) Clarence has a nightmare about Richard pushing him into the sea. Then two murderers — sent by Richard — stab him and drown him in a barrel of wine.

2) Stanley has a dream about how dangerous Richard is. He sends a messenger to warn Hastings, but Hastings laughs at it.

I predict you will pass your exams, oh yes...

Studying the play today, it's tempting to see Margaret's curses as just the rabid ramblings of a mad, bitter old hag. But in Shakespeare's times, they would have been seen as a grim warning.

Section 4 — Understanding The Story

Crimes, Guilt and Remorse

There's an awful lot of nastiness in this play. Some of the characters come to realise that murdering people just isn't cricket. Richard just ploughs on regardless though.

Bad Deeds Have Bad Consequences

In Shakespeare's time, people had strong ideas about good and evil. Most people in England were Christian and believed that, if you did bad things in this life, your soul would be punished when you died.

The play is full of characters who lie, trick each other and even kill. Shakespeare wanted us to see that they wouldn't be rewarded for it.

Don't say I didn't warn you, sunshine.

Some Characters Feel Guilty

Several characters want to clear their consciences before they die. They hope that if they repent their crimes they will save their souls from being damned forever.

1) Clarence has a horrible dream about drowning. He feels guilty because in the past he fought against his brother, Edward IV. He accepts that God may punish him for that. He prays that his family doesn't suffer for his crime though.

2) The murderers who come to kill Clarence don't find it easy. Clarence warns them that if they kill him they're breaking God's laws. The second murderer talks about his own conscience. He repents almost immediately.

3) Edward IV knows he's going to die. He's keen to do good before he dies so his soul will go to Heaven. He's full of remorse when he hears that Clarence has been killed. He's afraid God will judge them all for it.

4) Dighton and Forrest, who Tyrell gets to kill the Princes, end up weeping with guilt.

5) Buckingham has an attack of conscience too. Just before he's executed, he admits that he has done wrong. He says he deserves to die.

Richard III Isn't Sorry for What He's Done

In for a penny...

1) At the start of the play, Richard boasts about the trouble he's going to cause — and he does it. He chooses to be a villain right to the end.

2) Richard has more to feel guilty about than anyone. He's haunted by the ghosts of his victims just before the battle. He has to face up to what he's done.

3) It's a clear chance to repent. But he rejects his conscience and sticks with his plans.

Sorry is all that you can't say...

You might think that saying sorry just isn't good enough when you've done the things these people have done. But in Richard III, realising you've done wrong is a big thing. The fact that Richard never repents makes him come across as much, much worse than Buckingham or anyone else.

Section 4 — Understanding The Story

What Happens in Act One

ACT 1 SCENES 1 & 2

Right then. This is a long old play, so best get down to it and find out what happens.

Scene 1 — Richard Cons Clarence

Before the play starts, the royal houses of York and Lancaster have been at war. The Lancastrian King Henry VI and his son Prince Edward have been killed by Richard, a Yorkist. Now Richard's brother, Edward IV, is King, and the Yorkists are back in power. But the troubles are far from over...

1 The wars are over, but Richard's not happy
England is at peace, and now Edward IV, Richard's older brother, is King. But peace and happiness don't suit Richard — he says he's ugly and deformed, and determined to cause trouble. He tells us that he's turned King Edward and his other brother, the Duke of Clarence, against each other. Lines 1-41

He ain't heavy... he's my brother.

2 Richard tells Clarence he'll stick up for him
Clarence enters on his way to being imprisoned in the Tower of London. Richard pretends to be surprised and asks why Clarence is being imprisoned, and Clarence says he doesn't know. Richard then tells Clarence that it's not the King who's behind it, but his wife, Queen Elizabeth. Richard then tells Clarence that he'll stick up for him and get him freed (he's lying). The guard leads Clarence away, then Richard reveals he's actually going to have Clarence killed. Lines 42-120

3 Hastings tells Richard the King is ill
Hastings arrives and tells Richard that King Edward is sick and the doctors are very worried. Hastings leaves. Richard talks about his plan to get Clarence killed, and then marry Lady Anne. When King Edward IV dies, Richard wants to take his place. Lines 121-162

No one else hears Richard say this — it's his and our secret.

Scene 2 — Richard Chats Anne Up

1 Anne mourns for her husband and father-in-law
Anne follows the body of the former King, Henry VI, which is on its way to being buried. She mourns for him and for her husband, his son Prince Edward. Lines 1-32

2 Richard tries to woo Anne, but she resists
Richard enters and orders the procession to stop. Anne curses him, saying he killed Henry VI and Prince Edward. At first Richard denies it, then admits it. He cleverly tries to talk his way into Anne's affections, by saying that he killed them because Anne was so beautiful and he was in love with her. She spits at him and continues to curse him. Lines 33-150

3 Richard wins her over
Richard makes a speech about how he never cries, but he cries when he looks at Anne. He hands her his sword and tells her to kill him if she doesn't want him, but she won't kill him. He gives her a ring, and eventually manages to convince Anne to leave the procession and meet up with him later on. Lines 151-226

4 Richard congratulates himself
Richard reflects on what he has achieved, winning over Anne despite being ugly and having killed her husband and father-in-law. Lines 227-263

What do you get if you cross a leopard with Richard III?

Spotted Dick. Anyway, there you have it — all the fun of the first two scenes. Use these pages to get to know the story and your key scenes should start to make a whole lot more sense.

Section 4 — Understanding The Story

What Happens in Act One

ACT 1 SCENES 3 & 4

Here's the rest of Act 1. I hope you haven't become too fond of Clarence...

Scene 3 — Margaret Curses Everyone

In this scene, the bitter old Queen Margaret (Henry VI's widow) enters the fray. She causes a lot of trouble, but that sly old dog Richard uses this to his advantage.

1. **Queen Elizabeth's relatives comfort her**
   Rivers and Grey try to cheer Queen Elizabeth up by telling her the King will be better soon. She's worried about the prospect of Richard becoming her son's Protector when the King dies. Stanley (Earl of Derby) and Buckingham arrive and report that the King is on the mend and is keen to sort out the quarrels between Richard and the Queen's family. Lines 1-41

2. **Richard starts an argument**
   Richard enters and claims that people have been spreading lies about him, Clarence and Hastings. Elizabeth says he's just jealous because her family has come into power. Lines 42-109

3. **Queen Margaret has a go at everyone**
   Margaret sneaks in and hides unseen from the other characters. She says to herself that Elizabeth has taken her rightful position of Queen, and says Richard is a murderer. Lines 110-156

Richard's only pretending to be sympathetic with Margaret. It adds to his image of being a simple, straight-up bloke. He's secretly quite happy about the upset Margaret's caused.

4. **Margaret causes a stir**
   Margaret comes forward and says the others are all fighting over what is hers. She warns them about Richard, but Elizabeth won't listen. Margaret predicts that Elizabeth will wish she had listened to her. She tries to be friendly to Buckingham, but he sides with Richard. Margaret curses them all and leaves. Richard defends Margaret, then Catesby comes to call them all over to see the King. Lines 157-322

5. **Richard plans more trouble**
   Richard reflects on his plan to blame Clarence's imprisonment on Queen Elizabeth's relatives (Rivers, Grey and Dorset), and to set Stanley, Hastings and Buckingham against them for it. Two murderers enter and Richard gives them instructions to kill Clarence. Lines 323-354

Scene 4 — Clarence is Murdered

Poor old Clarence almost talks his way out of it — but there's no stopping Richard's schemes.

1. **Clarence describes a bad dream**
   In the Tower, Clarence tells his keeper that he's had a horrible dream. He dreamt that he and Richard were on a ship, Richard slipped and pushed him overboard, and that he drowned, and went to hell. The keeper stays with Clarence while he sleeps. Lines 1-75

2. **The murderers come to Clarence**
   Brakenbury enters. The murderers enter and give Brakenbury a warrant instructing him to leave Clarence in their charge. Brakenbury and the keeper leave. One of the murderers has doubts about killing Clarence, but the other murderer reminds him of the money and he agrees to go through with it. Lines 76-152

3. **Clarence tries to talk them out of it, but is killed**
   Clarence wakes up and sees the murderers. He thinks that Edward has sent them. He manages to talk one of them out of killing him, but the other stabs him from behind, then drowns him in a wine barrel. Lines 153-278

Oh, don't be such a meanie.

We're only earning a living.

Section 4 — Understanding The Story

Act 2, Scenes 1-4 — What Happens in Act Two

Here's the whole of Act 2. By this point, Richard's really starting to take control. Boo, hiss.

Scene 1 — All's Going Well... then Richard Turns Up

Richard wants conflict, so he sabotages the King's efforts to make peace.

1 King Edward gets everyone to make friends
Queen Elizabeth and her relatives make their peace with Buckingham and Hastings. The King, who is ill, is happy about this. Lines 1-44

2 Richard tells them Clarence is dead
Richard arrives and pretends to make friends with everyone too. Then he tells them that Clarence is dead, and everyone is astonished. Richard says that the King's reversal of the death sentence came too late. Lines 45-95

3 The King is distraught
The King is very upset at the death of Clarence, and asks why no one tried to talk him out of ordering Clarence's death. Richard tells Buckingham that Clarence's death was the fault of Queen Elizabeth's relatives. Lines 96-141

Come on guys, where's the love?

Scene 2 — The King is Dead

1 Clarence's kids ask some awkward questions
Clarence's two children ask the Duchess of York, their grandmother, about their father's death. Clarence's son says that Richard told him it was Elizabeth's fault, but the Duchess says Richard is a liar. Lines 1-33

2 Elizabeth announces that the King is dead
Queen Elizabeth arrives with her relatives, Rivers and Dorset, and tells them that King Edward IV is dead. They reflect on the deaths of Clarence and the King. Rivers reminds Elizabeth that her young son, Prince Edward, will now be King. Lines 34-95

3 Buckingham sends for Prince Edward
Richard and Buckingham arrive, and Buckingham orders for a small group of people to be sent to fetch the young Prince Edward to be crowned as King. Then Buckingham tells Richard that he'll arrange for the Prince to be separated from Elizabeth's relatives. Lines 96-154

Prince Edward is only a child. If he becomes King, Richard will be his Lord Protector — which means he's in charge.

Scene 3 — Some Citizens Chat About England's Future

Three citizens (ordinary people) discuss the recent news
One citizen says things will be fine under the new King. Another citizen says that Richard is dangerous, and likely to quarrel with Elizabeth's family. He says that having a child as King will cause trouble.

Scene 4 — The Woodvilles are Arrested

The Woodvilles are Queen Elizabeth's family.

1 The young Duke of York talks about Prince Edward
The Archbishop of York, the old Duchess of York, Elizabeth and the young Duke of York chat about the arrival of young Prince Edward. Lines 1-37

2 A messenger brings bad news
Rivers, Grey and Vaughan have been arrested by Richard and Buckingham. Elizabeth realises her family is in danger and she and the young Duke go to sanctuary, where they are safer. Lines 38-73

Section 4 — Understanding The Story

What Happens in Act Three

ACT 3 SCENES 1-3

Richard really starts to get a taste for murder in this act. If only Taggart was around.

Scene 1 — The Young Princes Arrive

1 Prince Edward isn't happy
The young Prince Edward is unhappy that his relatives are not with him. Richard tells him they are evil people, but the Prince isn't convinced. Hastings reports that Elizabeth is holding the Prince's brother, the young Duke of York, in sanctuary. Buckingham orders Cardinal Bourchier to fetch them by force. Lines 1-60

2 Richard, Prince Edward and the Duke of York have a chat
Richard suggests that Prince Edward should stay in the Tower for a few days. The two of them talk for a while, and Richard comments to himself on the Prince's cleverness. Then the young Duke of York arrives, and he too demonstrates his wit. Then the two Princes reluctantly go off to the Tower. Lines 61-150

3 Buckingham and Richard do more plotting
Buckingham sends Catesby to find out whether Hastings will support Richard's bid to be King. Richard tells Buckingham that if Hastings won't support him, he'll have him killed. Then Richard promises Buckingham he'll be made Earl of Hereford when Richard becomes King. Lines 151-200

Scene 2 — Hastings Ignores Stanley's Warning

Hastings **won't listen** to Stanley's friendly word of advice. Uh-oh.

I've never felt less likely to be executed in all my life...

1 A messenger arrives
Hastings is woken by a messenger from Stanley. He warns Hastings of the danger from Richard and suggests they go north together. Hastings says there's nothing to worry about and sends the messenger away. Lines 1-34

2 Hastings tells Catesby he won't support Richard
Catesby arrives and tells Hastings that Elizabeth's relatives are to be killed. Catesby asks Hastings if he'll support Richard's claim to be King — Hastings says he won't. Lines 35-56

3 Hastings says he's got nothing to worry about
Hastings tells Catesby that he's mates with Richard and Buckingham. Stanley enters and points out to Hastings that the same thing could happen to them as to Elizabeth's family. But Hastings says that they're perfectly safe because Richard likes them. Hastings then speaks to some other people, including Buckingham, who knows that Hastings will be killed. Lines 57-123

This is dramatic irony (see p.45). The audience knows that Richard's perfectly prepared to have Hastings killed. He should've listened to Stanley...

Scene 3 — The Woodvilles are Taken to be Killed

The doomed prisoners remember Margaret's curse
Ratcliffe leads Rivers, Grey and Vaughan to their execution. Grey says that Margaret's curse on them is coming true. Rivers hopes it comes true for Richard, Buckingham and Hastings too.

Richard's ma-king me a bit nervous...

I'm beginning to see a pattern here. Clarence was in Richard's way. He got killed. The Woodvilles were awkward. They got killed... Ah well, I'm sure he knows what he's doing.

Section 4 — Understanding The Story

Act 3, Scenes 4-7: What Happens in Act Three

Scene 4 — It All Goes Wrong for Hastings

1 Prince Edward's coronation is discussed
Hastings, Buckingham, Stanley and the Bishop of Ely meet to discuss the date of the coronation. The Bishop asks Buckingham's opinion, but Buckingham says that Hastings is closer to Richard than him. Richard enters and privately tells Buckingham that he's going to have Hastings killed. Hastings fails to see what's going on and says that Richard seems to be happy. Lines 1-57

2 Richard tricks Hastings
Richard says there's been a plot against him, and Hastings says whoever's behind it deserves to be killed. Richard says it's Elizabeth and Mistress Shore (Hastings' mistress) and orders the execution of Hastings. Hastings wishes he'd listened to Stanley's warnings. He realises Margaret's curse against him has come true. Ratcliffe and Lovell lead him away. Lines 58-107

Oops.

Richard can't just kill Hastings for no clear reason, so he makes it look like he's a traitor.

Scene 5 — Richard Prepares to Become King

Help! We're under attack!

Well I'm convinced. There's no way this is a trick, none at all.

1 Richard and Buckingham pretend to be under attack
Dressed up in armour, Richard and Buckingham make out to the Mayor that there's been a plot against them and that they're in danger of their lives. Lovell and Ratcliffe come in with Hastings' head. Richard pretends to be sad that Hastings is dead, but says he had no choice but to have him killed. The Mayor is fooled and goes to explain the situation to the citizens. Lines 1-71

2 Richard puts the final touches to his plan to be King
Richard tells Buckingham to tell the citizens that Edward's children, the young Princes, are illegitimate, meaning Richard should be King. Lines 72-109

Scene 6 — A Scrivener Speaks

A scrivener realises what's going on
A scrivener (legal writer) looks over a document accusing Hastings of being a traitor. He realises that the accusation is false, as he was given it the previous night, before Hastings was accused.

Scene 7 — Richard Becomes King

1 The citizens aren't keen
Buckingham tells Richard that he's tried to persuade the citizens of Richard's right to be King, but they weren't very enthusiastic about it. Buckingham tells Richard to pretend to be praying for when the Mayor arrives. Lines 1-55

2 Richard pretends to be reluctant
The Mayor and Catesby arrive. Catesby is sent to ask Richard to be King. Richard pretends to be busy praying and says he doesn't want to be King. Buckingham (who's in on the trick) and the Mayor (who isn't) eventually persuade Richard that he must become King. Lines 56-247

Section 4 — Understanding The Story

What Happens in Act Four

ACT 4 SCENES 1-3

OK, so Richard's an evil murderer hell-bent on power. But surely he's good with children?

Scene 1 — The Visitors are Denied Access to the Princes

1 Brakenbury says Elizabeth, Anne and the Duchess can't see the young Princes
Queen Elizabeth, the Duchess of York, Dorset and Lady Anne meet on their way to visit Prince Edward and the young Duke of York in the Tower. Then Brakenbury appears and tells them Richard won't allow it. The women protest but Brakenbury isn't having any of it. Stanley arrives to summon Anne to be crowned as Richard's Queen. Lines 1-27

2 Elizabeth, Anne and the Duchess are worried
The women realise that Richard is up to no good. Anne wishes she'd never agreed to marry Richard and says he will have her killed. The Duchess tells Dorset to leave and join Richmond, who is forming an army to fight Richard. The Duchess also tells Anne to go to Richard and Elizabeth to go to sanctuary. Lines 28-103

Scene 2 — King Richard Plans More Murders

1 The new King plots to kill the two young Princes
The newly crowned King Richard III takes the throne. He wants Prince Edward and the young Duke of York dead, and asks for Buckingham's help. Buckingham isn't sure and goes away to think about it. Lines 1-31

2 Richard hires Tyrrel to kill the Princes and plans Anne's death too
Richard sends a page to fetch a man called Tyrrel to kill the Princes. Stanley tells Richard that Dorset has gone to join forces with Richmond. Richard tells Catesby to tell people that his wife Anne is sick and about to die. Tyrrel arrives and Richard gives him instructions to kill the Princes. Lines 32-81

He wants Anne dead so he can marry his niece (Queen Elizabeth's daughter, Elizabeth) to strengthen his position as King.

3 Buckingham's out of favour
Buckingham returns and asks for the reward Richard promised him, but Richard keeps ignoring him. Buckingham remembers that Richard had Hastings killed when he fell out with him, and realises he has to get away from Richard before the same thing happens to him. Lines 82-121

Scene 3 — The Young Princes are Dead

1 The Princes are dead
Tyrrel says the people he hired to kill the Princes almost changed their minds before going through with the murders. Then he tells Richard the Princes are dead. Richard says that Anne too is now dead, so he can go after his niece Elizabeth, but he is worried that Richmond also wants to marry her. Lines 1-43

2 Richard prepares for battle
Ratcliffe brings news of how Richmond and Buckingham are raising armies in Brittany in France against Richard. Richard tells Ratcliffe to gather soldiers for his army. Lines 44-57

Stop it, you're killing me...

At least now Dickie's started killing a few people, it's easier to remember who everyone is. You can't help feeling sorry for the kids, but Hastings — he's just stupid and deserves it if you ask me.

Section 4 — Understanding The Story

ACT 4
SCENES 4 & 5

What Happens in Act Four

He may be King now, but things start getting a bit sticky for Dickie from now on.

Scene 4 — Richard Prepares for Battle

1 Margaret says "I told you so"
Margaret listens in on Elizabeth and the Duchess of York discussing how miserable they are about what's happened to their families. Then Margaret comes forward and takes satisfaction in having been right about their downfalls. Lines 1-125

Now who's mad?

2 Elizabeth and the Duchess have a go at Richard
Richard enters and Queen Elizabeth and the Duchess remind him of the murders he has committed. The Duchess says he will have a violent death. Lines 126-196

3 Richard asks Elizabeth to help him marry her daughter
Richard wants to marry Queen Elizabeth's daughter, also called Elizabeth, and asks her to help him. At first Elizabeth refuses, saying her daughter would never marry Richard because he has killed so many members of her family. Lines 197-290

4 Richard seems to convince Elizabeth
Richard says he can't change what he's done in the past, but says he can make up for Queen Elizabeth's sorrow at not having a son as King by making her daughter his Queen. They have a long argument, and Elizabeth mockingly reminds Richard of how untrustworthy he is. Eventually, though, he seems to convince her, and she leaves. Lines 291-430

5 Richard distrusts Stanley
Ratcliffe reports that Richmond's army is sailing from France and will be joined by Buckingham's army. Richard sends Catesby to the Duke of Norfolk to tell him to raise an army. Stanley arrives and tells Richard that Richmond is sailing to England to try and become King. Richard tells Stanley to summon his friends to Richard's side. Richard thinks Stanley might betray him and help Richmond instead, so he holds Stanley's son, George, as a hostage, to ensure Stanley's loyalty. Lines 431-497

6 Some messengers bring bad news
Three messengers announce there are armies ready to fight Richard in various parts of England, but another says that Buckingham's army has split up and Buckingham has disappeared. Catesby says that Buckingham has been captured, but Richmond has landed with a strong army. Richard says they have to stop talking and prepare for battle. Lines 498-538

Scene 5 — Stanley Secretly Sends Richmond his Support

Stanley double-crosses Richard — he'll have to be careful.

Stanley sends Richmond a message
Stanley tells Sir Christopher Urswick to tell Richmond that he can't openly support him because Richard is holding his son hostage. But he says to tell him that Queen Elizabeth wants her daughter to marry Richmond. Stanley gives Sir Christopher a letter assuring Richmond that he is on his side.

Section 4 — Understanding The Story

What Happens in Act Five

ACT 5 SCENES 1-3

Ooh it's the last act, I'm all excited. But look out, there's ghosts in this bit...

Scene 1 — Buckingham's for the Chop

Buckingham is led to his execution
The sheriff takes Buckingham to be killed, telling him Richard won't speak with him. Buckingham realises he's getting what he deserves, and remembers Margaret's prophecy.

So Margaret was right about me too. Pants.

Scene 2 — Richmond's Feeling Confident

We've heard all about him — now Richmond finally makes an appearance.

Right, chaps, let's kick some hunchback bottom.

Richmond marches to battle
Richmond and his supporters are marching towards battle, and are only one day's march away from Richard. Richmond has received Stanley's letter of support, and he's feeling good.

Scene 3 — The Night Before Battle

1 Richard and Richmond set up camp
Richard's side pitch their tent in Bosworth field, ready for the battle the next morning. Richard says their army is three times as big as Richmond's. Nearby, Richmond arrives with his followers. He sends Blunt to find Stanley and give him a note. Lines 1-45

2 Richard sends for Stanley
It is the evening before the battle and Richard is feeling tense. He tells Catesby to send for Stanley's regiment, then talks with Ratcliffe about preparations for the battle. Lines 46-79

3 Stanley talks secretly with Richmond
Stanley wishes Richmond good luck, but explains that he cannot be seen supporting him because of Stanley's son being held hostage. Richmond prays then sleeps. Lines 80-118

4 The Ghosts of Richard's victims visit Richard and Richmond
The ghosts of the people Richard has murdered come to Richard and Richmond in their dreams — first the older Prince Edward, then Henry VI, Clarence, Rivers, Grey and Vaughan, Hastings, the two young Princes, Anne and finally Buckingham. The ghosts wish despair and death on Richard, and success and victory on Richmond. Richard wakes up terrified and feels haunted by his conscience. Ratcliffe comes to tell Richard the battle is about to begin. Lines 119-223

5 Richmond and Richard rouse their troops
Richmond wakes after having pleasant dreams. He gives an oration (speech) to his soldiers. Then Richard gives his oration to his troops. A messenger tells Richard that Stanley won't support him. Richard orders the death of Stanley's son, but there isn't time before the battle. Lines 224-352

Richard and Richmond use these speeches to motivate their troops before the big battle — doubtless accompanied by lots of "hurrahs" and "huzzahs".

Section 4 — Understanding The Story

What Happens in Act Five

ACT 5 SCENES 4 & 5

Nearly finished. I wonder how it'll end — maybe there'll be a really surprising twist...
Nope, the good guy wins. Never saw that coming.

Scene 4 — The Battle

He may be a scheming, dishonest murderer, but Richard's a brave fighter.

Richard looks for Richmond

In the midst of battle, Catesby and Norfolk come across Richard. His horse has been killed, but he's desperate for another one so he can go and fight Richmond, after having already killed five other men dressed like him. Catesby advises him to flee, but Richard is determined to fight Richmond.

COME ON THEN!

This is where Richard says the famous line "A horse, a horse, my kingdom for a horse!" In fact, he says it twice — it's that good.

Scene 5 — Richmond Defeats Richard

Richard finally meets his end — and not a second too soon.

1. **Richmond kills Richard**
   Richard and Richmond fight, and Richmond kills Richard. Stanley congratulates him and presents him with the crown, taken from Richard's head. Stanley tells us that his son is safe and well. Lines 1-14

2. **Richmond looks forward to peace**
   In the closing speech, Richmond says he will bring together the warring sides of the royal family. He says he'll unite the houses of York and Lancaster by marrying the Yorkist Princess Elizabeth (Richmond is a Lancastrian), so that England can be peaceful again. Lines 15-41

Now let's jolly well live in peace together, what?

That's all folks...

Come on, admit it, it's not that boring. There's loads of action, and all that double-dealing certainly keeps it interesting. If you ever get in a muddle while you're reading the play, you can always have a look back at this section to work out what's happening. Now, unto the exam, and victory! Ahem.

Section 4 — Understanding The Story

Revision Summary

I told you it was a long play. It's complicated too, and right now you're probably feeling exhausted just from trying to follow it. But it'll all click into place in time. And luckily for you, I've written loads of questions about what happens, so you can see what you know and what you don't. Take a deep breath and dive in.

1) Who were the two sides in the Wars of the Roses?
   a) The Houses of York and Lancaster.
   b) Britain and France.
   c) Chelsea and Arsenal.
2) What's the "Tudor Myth"?
3) What's the first prophecy mentioned in the play?
4) What does Queen Margaret say about the young Prince Edward?
5) When does Buckingham realise he's done wrong?
6) How does Richard react to his chance to repent?
7) Who's the King at the start of the play?
8) Who's being led to the Tower in Act 1, Scene 1?
9) Who does Richard blame Clarence's imprisonment on?
10) Who is Anne mourning for when Richard interrupts her?
11) What does Clarence dream about before he's murdered?
    a) The deaths of the young Princes.
    b) Drowning and going to hell.
    c) A tractor made of spaghetti.
12) How does Richard ruin King Edward IV's attempts to create peace?
13) Why would Richard gain more power if Prince Edward became King?
14) Which characters are arrested in Act 2, Scene 4?
15) What does Richard promise Buckingham as a reward for his support?
16) What's Hastings' reaction to Stanley's warning?
17) How does Richard trick Hastings in Act 3, Scene 4?
18) Who does Richard get to tell the people that the young Princes are illegitimate?
19) Why does the Scrivener reckon the accusation against Hastings is dodgy?
20) What's Richard doing when the Mayor comes to ask him to be King?
21) Who prevents the women from visiting the young Princes in the Tower?
22) What's Buckingham's response when Richard asks for his support in killing the young Princes?
23) What does Richard ask of Queen Elizabeth in Act 4, Scene 4?
24) How does Richard try to make sure Stanley's loyal to him?
25) What does Stanley tell Richmond in his message in Act 4, Scene 5?
26) What effect do the ghosts have on Richard and Richmond?
27) Why does Richard want a horse in Act 5, Scene 4?
28) What does Richmond say he's going to do after becoming King?

Section 4 — Understanding The Story

SECTION 5 — WRITING AN ESSAY

Three Steps for an Essay

So you've had a good look at the play. In this section we'll look at the kind of essay you'll have to write, and some good tips for getting really good marks in the test.

Three Steps to Exam Success

These three steps are a little treasure for answering exam questions. And they work for any kind of Shakespeare question — bargain.

1) Read the question and underline the important bits.
2) Go through the set scenes and look for examples you could use in your answer.
3) Do a quick plan for your essay. Look back at this when you're writing so you don't run out of ideas.

See pages 33-34 for more about planning.

The Question Will Look Like This

Whichever question type you get, the basic layout will look like this:

Richard III

Act 1 Scene 3, lines 130-214
Act 5 Scene 3, lines 119-177

In these scenes, Queen Margaret argues with Richard and the ghosts of Richard's victims appear in a dream.

How does the language in these scenes create a tense atmosphere?

Support your ideas by referring to both of the extracts which are printed on the following pages.

18 marks

There might be a bit like this to introduce the topic of the question.

This bit tells you which parts of the play the question is about. It'll be about half the set scenes (printed on pages 49-56 of this book).

This basically means "keep looking at the scenes and include loads of quotes".

This is the really important bit — the actual question. It's important that you read this carefully, so that you fully understand what you're being asked.

Steps? I thought they'd split up...

Although there are a few different types of question (see Section 6), they all pretty much follow the same format as the one on this page. So get familiar with it and you'll know what to expect.

Using Quotes

For every point you make, you have to back it up by using a quote. Quotes prove your points — if you don't use them, you've got no proof that you're not just making it up.

Keep the Quotes Short

Keep quotes short and to the point — a couple of lines is usually enough.

e.g. Queen Margaret clearly hates Richard. While watching him arguing with Elizabeth, Margaret makes several comments about him, unheard by the other characters, which suggest a bitter argument is to come:
"Hie thee to hell for shame, and leave this world,
Thou cacodemon! there thy kingdom is."   Act 1, Scene 3, 142-143

Start a new paragraph.

Copy down the exact words.

Say where the quote comes from. Give the act, scene, and line numbers.

If the quote's less than a line you don't need to put it in a separate paragraph or say where the quote's from, but you do need to put it in speech marks.

e.g. Richard is just as insulting to Margaret as she is to him. He responds to her comments by calling her a "hateful withered hag".

Explain Why the Quote is Relevant

1) Remember to make it really clear why you've included the quotes — don't just stick them in and expect the examiner to see the point you're making.

e.g. Clarence's ghost reminds Richard of how he was "betrayed to death". This brings up the subject of Richard's crimes, suggesting he will pay for them. When each ghost tells him to "despair and die", it seems Richard is doomed, further adding to the tension before the battle.

These quotes are good because they show something about the atmosphere of the scene, which is what the question's about.

2) Quote different characters — this makes your answer more interesting. E.g. Even before Margaret joins in, there's already a bitter row between Richard and Queen Elizabeth, so you could quote some of this.

3) Remember that characters will have particular reasons for saying certain things — think about why they say them and the effect of the quote.

Status Quote — the studious rock band...

So the main points about quoting are: 1) Keep 'em short. 2) Explain how they answer the question. This'll make sure the quotes really add something to your answer.

Section 5 — Writing an Essay

Planning and Structure

If you plan your essay first, you'll have more chance of getting loads of marks.

You Need a Beginning, a Middle and an End

A good essay has a beginning, a middle and an end. Just like a good story.

Just like me then.

1) The hardest part is beginning your essay. The first sentence has to start answering the question, and tell the examiner that your essay is going to be good. All that from one sentence — so you'd better start practising.

2) The middle part of your essay develops your argument — this is where you make all your points. Follow your plan.

3) The end sums up the points you've made and rounds the essay off nicely.

Before You Write, Make a Plan

Planning means organising your material to help you write a clear answer that makes sense. A good plan turns that heap of ideas in your head into an argument supported by points.

I wish I was organised...

Planning might seem a pain to do, but if you do it, you'll be less likely to get lost halfway through the essay.

Five Steps to Planning a Good Essay

1) Work out exactly what the question is asking you to do. Find the key words and underline them.

2) Read the set scenes — highlight quotations you could use.

3) Jot down your ideas — from the set scenes they give you, and from your knowledge of the rest of the play — and then put them into an order.

4) Decide what your opinion is, and how you can use your points to support it — to form an argument. Put your best point first.

5) Don't stick to your plan rigidly. If you think of any more good ideas once you've started writing, then try to fit them in.

It's the beginning of the end...

If you're not sure what your opinion is, state the arguments for and against, and give evidence to support each viewpoint. Answer the question by comparing the views on each side.

Section 5 — Writing an Essay

Planning and Structure

Here's an <u>example</u> of how you could make a plan for a question on Richard III.

Work Out What the Question is Asking

e.g. Act 1 Scene 2, lines 153-229 and Act 3 Scene 5, lines 1-71
In these scenes Richard wins Anne over and fools the Lord Mayor.
What do we learn about the character of Richard from these scenes?
Support your ideas by referring to the scenes.

1) Start by <u>underlining</u> the most <u>important</u> words in the question.
   For this one you'd underline "character" and "Richard".

2) Once you've got the question in your head, go through the scenes and <u>pick out sections</u> of the scenes that look like they'll help your answer.

> Teach not thy lip such scorn; for it was made
> For kissing, lady, not for such contempt.
> Act 1, Scene 2, 171-172

3) Go through the scenes again and check for things you <u>might have missed</u> —
   it looks really good if you can find points that are <u>relevant</u> but <u>not obvious</u>.

Making Your Plan

Next jot down a <u>plan</u> for your essay. <u>Don't</u> bother writing in proper English in your plan — just get your ideas down.

This essay is all about <u>Richard</u>, so make notes on <u>anything</u> from the scenes you think tells us something about Richard.

Decide on the best <u>order</u> for your points.

Write down any <u>comments</u> you've got on what happens.

Find some <u>good quotes</u> to back up your points.

<u>Richard's character</u>

1. <u>He's very determined</u> He persuades Anne to marry him, even though she at first hates and insults him — "Teach not thy lip such scorn".

3. 2. <u>He's proud of his skills</u> At the end of Act 1 Scene 2, he is very pleased with himself for winning Anne against all the odds — "Was ever woman in this humour won?"

2. 3. <u>He's clever and good with words</u> He sets up a complicated plan to trick the Mayor. He dresses up in armour and pretends to be under attack, and fools the Mayor with his acting — "Look back! Defend thee!"

My essay blossomed — I plant it well...

<u>Don't</u> just launch straight in — take the <u>time</u> to plan. Once you've <u>jotted</u> some ideas down, you'll realise you have <u>more</u> to say than you thought — so there's <u>less</u> reason to <u>panic</u>. And let's face it, a <u>structured</u> essay will get more marks than one that goes <u>all over the place</u>...

Section 5 — Writing an Essay

Writing Your Answer

Once you've got a plan, you're ready to start writing.
Make your points as clearly as you can so the examiner knows what you're on about.

Write a Simple Opening Paragraph

Start by using the exact words of the task in your introduction.
This shows you've understood the question.

Your introduction doesn't have to be long at all. It's just there to show what your basic answer to the task is. In the rest of the paragraphs you'll need to go into detail.

e.g.
> What do we learn about the character of Richard from these scenes?
>
> In these scenes, we learn several things about Richard. In successfully wooing Anne, and winning the support of the Lord Mayor, Richard shows that he is a clever, determined character who is proud of his skills.
>
> The first thing we notice from these extracts is ...

The opening sentences use words from the question.

Once you've written your opening paragraph, just follow the order of your plan to write the rest of your essay.

Make Your Answer Interesting

1) Use interesting words — the examiner will get bored if you overuse dull words and phrases like "nice" and "I think". Try using words like "fascinating" and phrases like "in my opinion".

2) Keep your style formal — write in full sentences and don't use slang words. This makes your argument more convincing and gets you even more marks.

3) If you think a passage is "poetic", "realistic" etc., remember to explain exactly why — with examples. Don't assume it's obvious to the examiner.

Keep bearing in mind the words used in the question. Using them in your essay will show you're keeping to the task and not getting lost.

Allow me to introduce my lovely essay...

Your intro really doesn't need to be anything mindblowing. Just a couple of sentences to show you've understood the question and to get your answer started. Then you start moving onto more detailed points in the rest of your answer, with some nice tasty quotes to back them up.

Section 5 — Writing an Essay

Concluding and Checking for Errors

Once you've made all your points, you need to sum up your answer and check it through.

Write a Conclusion to Sum Up Your Key Points

The conclusion to my speech will be very concise — barely half an hour...

1) Start a new paragraph for your conclusion.

2) Sum up the main points of your essay briefly. This makes it clear how you've answered the question.

3) Don't go on and on, though. It's best if your conclusion is just a couple of sentences.

Go Over Your Essay When You've Finished

1) Try to leave time at the end to read through your essay quickly. Check that it makes sense, that you haven't got any facts wrong, and that it says what you want it to say.

How many more times do I have to go over it?

2) Check the grammar, spelling and punctuation. If you find a mistake, put brackets round it, cross it out neatly with two lines through it and write the correction above.

Don't scribble or put whitener on mistakes — it looks messy and you'll lose marks.

> determined
> Richard is (diturmined) to be King

3) If you've written something which isn't clear, put an asterisk * at the end of the sentence. Put another asterisk in the margin, and write what you mean in the margin.

> *He holds his son hostage. | Richard does not trust Stanley*.

Don't Panic if You Realise You've Gone Wrong

If you realise you've forgotten something really obvious and easy, then write a note about it at the bottom of the final page, to tell the examiner. If there's time, write an extra paragraph. You'll pick up marks for noticing your mistake.

> Don't give up if you're running out of time — even if you only have five minutes left, that's still time to pick up extra marks.

Check, check, check — I must be rich...

You've almost finished. Keep your conclusions to the point, and check your essay so you don't throw away marks on silly mistakes. Keep a clear head right up to the end — then it's teatime.

Section 5 — Writing an Essay

Revision Summary

I like to think of it as the 5 Ps — Planning Prevents Pitifully Poor Performance. Actually, I think it's a bit more positive than that — Planning Provides Practically Perfect Performance. The main point is Planning Planning Planning Planning Planning. Anyway, that's enough Ps for now.
On with the revision summary — you only know the answers when you don't have to flick back.

1) Name three useful things you should do before you start writing an answer to an exam question.
2) Why is it important to use lots of quotes in your essay?
3) What three bits of information do you have to give after any quote that's more than a line long?
4) What type of punctuation marks should you use on quotes that are shorter than one line?
5) What should you explain about every quote you use?
6) Which of the following are the three vital ingredients of a good essay?
   a) Spelling, handwriting and punctuation.
   b) Great ideas, brilliant ideas and fantastic ideas.
   c) A beginning, a middle and an end.
7) What's the big advantage of making a plan for an essay question?
8) If you have a great idea when you're writing your essay, which wasn't on your original plan, is it OK to fit it into your essay anyway?
9) How important is it to write your plan in proper English?
10) What do you have to do with the first sentence of your answer?
    a) Give a general answer to the question.
    b) Make your best point straightaway.
    c) Put in a really interesting quote.
11) Should you use mostly formal language or mostly slang in your answer?
12) How long should your closing paragraph be?
    a) About half a page.
    b) As long as a piece of string.
    c) As short as possible but including all the main points from your essay.
13) Write down four things you should check for when you read through your essay at the end.
14) How do you correct a spelling mistake?
15) What should you do if you've written something which isn't clear?

Section 5 — Writing an Essay

SECTION 6 — TYPES OF QUESTION

CHARACTER QUESTIONS

Questions About a Character

You might be asked a question about a particular character in Richard III.

Character Questions are Fairly Simple

Questions about a character will often ask you what the scenes show about that person.

> **e.g.** Act 1 Scene 3 and Act 3 Scene 7
> In these scenes we learn about Richard's character.
> **How is Richard shown to be a dishonest character?**
> *Support your ideas by referring to the scenes.*

Start by underlining the most important words in the question — you can write on the exam paper.

> How is Richard shown to be a dishonest character?

You have to explain how Shakespeare lets the audience know Richard's a trickster.

The underlined words are the most important ones. They tell you what to write about.

Remember Who's In Favour and Who's Not

People fall in and out of Richard's favour throughout the play. It's important to remember whether the character you're writing about is on Richard's side or against him, as this will affect the character's behaviour.

1) Hastings thinks Richard likes him, but then Richard goes and has him executed.
2) Richard goes out of his way to get Anne as his Queen, then has her killed when he decides he wants to marry his niece instead. Men eh?
3) Buckingham is Richard's right-hand man for a long time. He's loyal to Richard and helps him to become King. But even Buckingham ends up running for his life — unsuccessfully.

There are Loads of Characters in this Play

It's easy to think, "Blimey, I'll never remember who all these people are". It's true that there are lots of characters, but the more you study the play, the more they all fit into place.

This is why it's dead important that you know what happens in the whole play — if you only read the set scenes, you won't know who's who or what they're up to.

> Have a good look at pages 9-16 for more details on the characters.
> Read pages 21-29 for a summary of what happens in the whole play.

That Richard, eh? What a character...

These questions shouldn't ask you anything unexpected — you should know about the characters and their odd little ways before the exam. Try to be really thorough and there'll be no hiccups.

Section 6 — Types of Question

Characters — The Bigger Picture

CHARACTER QUESTIONS

If you're asked to write about a character there are a few things you can do to get more marks — it's a question of looking for the less obvious things.

Some Characters are Complicated

1) Shakespeare's characters aren't always everything that they seem — if they were, they'd be pretty boring. Take Richard — he's constantly pretending to be something he's not, and he's very good at it.

> And therefore, since I cannot prove a lover
> To entertain these fair well-spoken days,
> I am determined to prove a villain
> And hate the idle pleasures of these days.
> *Act 1, Scene 1, 28-31*

2) The audience know what he's doing though because he says at the start that he's up to no good.

3) Keep in mind what characters are trying to achieve, e.g. Richard really wants to become King, and he's prepared to lie and kill in order to achieve his goal.

It's a fair cop.

4) Some characters are mostly bad but have a few good qualities, e.g. Buckingham accepts his fate when he comes to have his head chopped off.

Think About What Motivates the Characters

1) Motivation means the reasons a character has for acting as they do.

2) The characters in Richard III are all after different things. Some people are driven by good intentions, some by bad intentions. Some of them do things for themselves, some do things for others.

3) Try to show in your answer that you understand what motivates the character you're writing about. Find a good quote and say what it tells you about the character:

e.g.
> Although Richard convinces many other characters that he has good intentions, the audience know this is not the case. At the start of the play, Richard says quite clearly that his motivation is purely to cause trouble.
>
> He is convinced that his ugly appearance means he "cannot prove a lover" or take any pleasure from doing good deeds. Instead, he intends to do what comes naturally, and simply "prove a villain".

Bill Shakes-beer — the nervous pub landlord...

So that's one type of exam question. Writing about characters is probably the simplest of the four kinds of question you might get. On the next two pages we'll look at writing about language.

Section 6 — Types of Question

LANGUAGE QUESTIONS

How Language is Used

If you're asked about Shakespeare's "use of language", it just means which words he uses.

Language Can Tell us About Characters

The kind of words each character uses affects our impression of them.

1) Queen Margaret's speeches are generally full of insults and curses. This creates an impression of her being very bitter.

> Thou elvish-marked, abortive, rooting hog!
> Thou that wast sealed in thy nativity
> The slave of nature and the son of hell!
> Act 1, Scene 3, 227-229

2) Richard's clever use of language is a big part of his character. Despite his ugliness and all the people who hate him, he smooth-talks his way to marrying Anne. His way with words is part of what makes him so clever.

3) The language the young Prince Edward uses is important. He's a clever child who's good at arguing, and so Richard realises he could be a threat to his ambitions to be King.

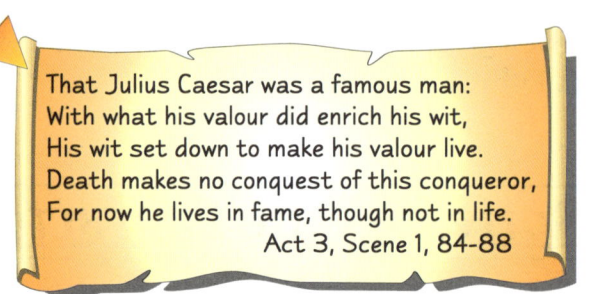

> That Julius Caesar was a famous man:
> With what his valour did enrich his wit,
> His wit set down to make his valour live.
> Death makes no conquest of this conqueror,
> For now he lives in fame, though not in life.
> Act 3, Scene 1, 84-88

What a clever boy you are...

Must kill the boy...

4) But the way Prince Edward talks also shows he's innocent and naive — he calls Richard his "uncle Gloucester" — which makes it all the more brutal when Richard has him and his brother killed.

Language Can Be Misleading

1) People don't always mean what they say. Just like in real life, the characters in Richard III can be sarcastic, secretive, unclear, or just plain lying.

2) Characters can say things in different ways in the same scene. E.g. In Act 1 Scene 1, when Richard tells Clarence he'll try and help him out, he's pretending to be nice. But when Richard's on his own, he says what he really thinks.

3) When you write about language, you have to show you understand what a character is really saying. Don't assume the examiner will realise you know — make it nice and clear.

As long as it's not in Swedish, you'll be fine...

Studying Shakespeare is really all about looking at what language he uses. So if you get a question that asks you specifically about his choice of words, there should be plenty you can write about.

Section 6 — Types of Question

How Language Creates Mood

LANGUAGE QUESTIONS

"Mood" or "atmosphere" means the <u>feel</u> of a scene — whether it's tense, funny, exciting or whatever. You might be asked about <u>how language is used</u> to create a particular <u>mood</u>.

Say What **Effect** the Words Create

e.g. Act 1 Scene 3 and Act 2 Scene 1
How does Shakespeare use language to create a mood of suspense and hostility?

Tense and hostile... How about some snakes? No...

Use words from the question.

> Shakespeare creates a mood of suspense and hostility through his use of aggressive, angry language. At first, Margaret lurks in the background, unseen by the other characters. She makes scathing aside comments about them, such as "Thou cacodemon!", referring to Richard. This creates suspense because we know that when she comes forward there will be trouble.
>
> Margaret's language is full of bitter, violent feelings. For example, she calls the other characters "wrangling pirates", showing that she distrusts them and sees them as criminals fighting over her rightful position. Richard's response of "foul wrinkled witch" adds to the sense of hostility between the characters.

Explain the exact effect of the language.

Explain your points — use "because".

Keep the answer focused and to-the-point.

Quote loads.

Look for **Mood Changes** Within Scenes

It'll add a little <u>extra</u> to your answer if you can identify the place where the mood of a scene <u>changes</u>. For example, if you were writing about Act 2, Scene 1, you could say something like:

> When King Edward says "A pleasing cordial" in Act 2 Scene 1, he seems satisfied and relieved. At this point the mood is relaxed and happy, with Queen Elizabeth's family making peace with Buckingham and Hastings.
>
> However, the mood becomes much darker when Richard announces Clarence's death. When King Edward asks who "Kneeled at my feet and bid me be advised?", he sounds very regretful and angry.

Show how the language reflects the change.

Say where the change in mood happens.

Heaven knows I'm miserable now... but not now...

So there's quite a bit you can write about for these questions to please the examiner. They give you the opportunity to really go to town and show off your <u>understanding</u> of the language.

Section 6 — Types of Question

THEME QUESTIONS

Writing About a Theme

Theme questions sound more tricky than they really are. They're generally just asking <u>how</u> the play puts across a particular <u>message, idea</u> or <u>issue</u>.

Work Out What the Question is Asking

Theme questions are often worded like this:

> Act 1 Scene 1, lines 1-43 and Act 4 Scene 2, lines 1-64
>
> In these scenes, Richard plots the deaths of Clarence, the young Princes and his wife Anne.
>
> **How do these extracts present the idea that Richard is both intelligent and evil?**
>
> *Support your ideas by referring to the scenes.*

Don't panic if the question seems complicated.

Read it carefully, and you'll realise it's actually pretty <u>simple</u>. Remember to <u>underline</u> the key words to help you work out what it's asking.

> You could rephrase this as:
> "These bits of the play show that Richard is both intelligent and evil. How do they do this?"

Theme Questions Aren't as Hard as They Look

1) Read through the scenes with the question in mind, and some points should pretty much <u>leap out</u> at you and give you the <u>basis for a good answer</u>. For example, for the question above, this quote from <u>Richard</u> would be useful:

> I must be married to my brother's daughter,
> Or else my kingdom stands on brittle glass:
> Murder her brothers, and then marry her —
> Uncertain way of gain! But I am in
> So far in blood that sin will pluck on sin.
> Tear-falling pity dwells not in this eye.
>   Act 4, Scene 2, 59-64

> To-do list
> 1) Murder nephews.
> 2) Sort out Buckingham.
> 3) Murder the wife.
> 4) Marry the niece.
> 5) Re-tile bathroom.

2) Once you've found a good extract like this, just say <u>how it relates to the question</u>. Don't forget to stick in some good <u>quotes</u> to back up your points:

> *Richard is fully aware that what he is doing is wrong, but scorns the idea of having "Tear-falling pity" for his victims. However, despite his arrogance and ruthlessness, he knows that his "kingdom stands on brittle glass". He is clever enough to realise that he needs to strengthen his position as King.*

I don't like extracts — they remind me of dentists...

Questions about themes generally <u>tell you</u> an opinion, then ask you to <u>prove</u> that it's true. Which makes it <u>easy</u> really — no faffing about deciding what to argue, just find some good <u>evidence</u>.

Section 6 — Types of Question

Themes You Might be Asked About

THEME QUESTIONS

Here's a few more things you can do if you get a question about a theme or issue in Richard III.

There are Several Themes in Richard III

If you do get a theme question, it's likely to be about one of these:

- good and evil
- royalty
- dreams and omens
- crimes and guilt
- loyalty
- history

It's worth having a think about these themes and working out what you'd write about them. Have a look at pages 18-20 for more about the themes in Richard III.

Look for the Less Obvious Bits

1) There will usually be plenty of fairly obvious points you can use in your answer to a theme question.

2) But if you want to get really great marks, you'll need to go into a bit more detail. Try to write something that answers the question in a way that's not immediately obvious.

> **e.g.** *Although Richard is a cold-blooded murderer, we cannot help admiring his cleverness and cunning. He has thought out exactly how to achieve his goals, using a combination of "inductions dangerous" and "drunken prophecies". The fact that he manages to rise to the position of King, despite being hated by so many powerful people, shows how cleverly he carries out his plan and how determined he is.*

3) It's especially important that you give evidence for these kinds of points. The examiner might not have thought of this, so it's vital that you back it up with good quotations.

4) Don't go over the top trying to write blindingly original stuff — make sure you don't miss out the clear-cut points that'll give you easy marks. But if you can stick just one or two more unexpected, well-explained points into your plan, along with the easier stuff, they'll make your answer really stand out.

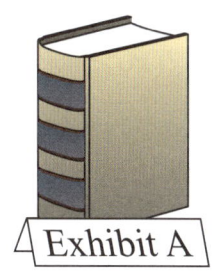

Exhibit A

> Make sure you stick to the question — it's easy to go off the point when you're trying to come up with a really original answer.

Where do topics go to have fun? A theme park...

You'll never get a question that asks you something unexpected, like "Explore how Richard III suggests that life is all about eating squid". It'll always be a fairly obvious theme, so don't worry.

Section 6 — Types of Question

DIRECTING QUESTIONS

Directing a Scene

The fourth type of exam question you might get asks you to imagine you're a director — the person who's in charge of the performance of the play.

As a Director You Can be Creative

If you get a question on how you'd direct a scene, it's a good opportunity to use your imagination. It's all about how to make the play look and sound great on stage. Here's an example question:

> Act 2 Scene 1, lines 74-end of scene and Act 3 Scene 2, lines 35-95
>
> Imagine you are directing a production of *Richard III*.
>
> **How would you direct the actors playing Richard, King Edward, Hastings and Catesby in these scenes?**
>
> *Explain your ideas with references to the extracts.*

Use the Language and Stage Directions

These questions can be a bit scary if you're struggling to think of good ideas. But there will be plenty of clues in the text which will give you some ideas.

1) Look for LINES that stand out

Find some lines that sound dramatic — happy, angry, scary, anything emotional.

Then think about how the actor should say these lines to really give them impact.

2) Look for STAGE DIRECTIONS

These hint at what's happening on stage — e.g. who's moving where, or what sounds and lighting there are.

You can interpret these — say how you'd make them happen.

e.g.

In my opinion, when Hastings says, "I shall laugh at this", he should sound very relaxed. This would add to the sense that he does not realise the danger he is in.

When Catesby says the aside, "For they account his head upon the bridge", he should walk to the front of the stage, stare out at the audience and talk in a whisper, to create a sinister atmosphere.

— Quote
— What you'd do
— Why you'd do it
— Quote
— What you'd do
— Why you'd do it

Die-rector — threatening a clergyman?

As with the other questions, you don't have to come up with loads of really groundbreaking ideas. Just give some well-explained suggestions with the odd more detailed point and you're well away.

Section 6 — Types of Question

How the Characters Should Speak

DIRECTING QUESTIONS

It's fair to say that the most important thing about Shakespeare is the words he uses. So as a director, you have to help the actors get the meaning of these words across to the audience.

Actors Can Say Their Lines in Different Ways

1) Have a think about the meaning of the lines, then decide how you can get this across to the audience. It's all to do with tone of voice — e.g. angry, friendly, sarcastic.

2) There's no right or wrong answer. As long as you explain why you think an actor should speak in a certain way, and give some evidence from the play, you can't go wrong.

3) You can even suggest more than one way for the actor to speak a line — the examiner will like this, as it shows you're thinking really hard about the play. Just make sure you give reasons for each suggestion you make.

e.g. In Act 2 Scene 1, when King Edward says, "Is Clarence dead? The order was reversed." he is shocked by Richard's news. The actor could show this by *saying this line slowly and quietly, his voice shaking*.

On the other hand, he could shout this line, looking around him for someone to blame. This would show the anger and confusion caused by Richard's scheming.

- Give an idea about how the lines should be said.
- Give another opinion if you have one.
- Always explain why you have a certain idea. This is the most important part of your answer.

You Can Create a Sense of Anticipation

1) Anticipation means wanting to know what will happen next. Shakespeare sometimes creates a feeling of anticipation by letting the audience know something the characters don't — this is called dramatic irony.

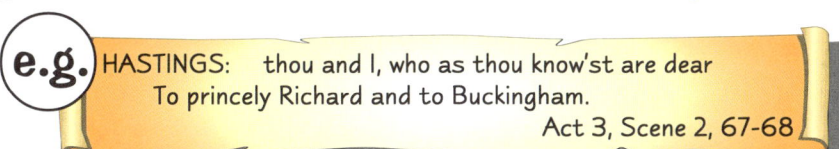

e.g.
> HASTINGS: thou and I, who as thou know'st are dear
> To princely Richard and to Buckingham.
> Act 3, Scene 2, 67-68

What's going on?

Ant is a patient.

2) Here, Hastings tells Catesby that he's mates with Richard. But we, the audience, have heard Richard say that he'll chop off Hastings' head if he steps out of line — and sure enough, that's what happens.

3) When writing as a director, you can say how you'd add to the suspense of the scene. E.g. For the bit above, after Hastings says these lines, Catesby could pause for a second before responding, to show he knows what's really going on.

Shtop! Thish play is not ready yet...

Being a director means giving your own interpretation of the play. Keep thinking about the effect you want to create on the audience — they're what it's all about. And be enthusiastic — it works.

Section 6 — Types of Question

DIRECTING QUESTIONS
How the Characters Should Act

The director can also create mood for the audience by thinking about how to get the actors to act and move.

Think About How Different Characters Will Act

Different characters will act in different ways in a scene. You can compare the way different characters act to show how mood is put across to the audience.

e.g. *Although King Edward is shocked, Richard knows exactly what is going on, and would sound calmer.* However, Richard could say the line "But he, poor man, by your first order died", in a reflective, regretful tone, *to show that he is pretending to be sad about Clarence's death.*

- Show that you know they don't all feel the same.
- Here's your explanation again — really important.

Think about how the characters are feeling, then how to show this in their tone of voice. And remember you can compare different characters and their feelings in the same scene.

Tell the Actors How to Move

They're actors, so make 'em act. Their body language — gestures, posture, movement — has a big effect on how their characters come across, and you can suggest things that aren't in the stage directions. As ever, explain your ideas and stick to the evidence in the play.

e.g. In Act 1 Scene 3, the actor playing Margaret should at first crouch near the back of the stage, *to show she is hiding from the other characters.* Then, when she comes forward, she should stride boldly into the middle of the stage. *In my opinion*, when she says "But repetition of what thou hast marred", she should turn violently towards Richard and *stab her finger in his chest, to show her hatred and aggression towards him.*

- Describe the effect you're trying to create.
- Use phrases like "in my opinion" — they show it's your idea.
- Expand on your idea.

If you talk about two different ideas about how to direct a scene, your answer will look better if you link your points together.

Linking words are dead useful. They help you move from one part of your answer to the next.

Some good linking words are:
- however
- on the other hand
- although
- in comparison

Get your act together...

So there's a lot to think about in these what-if-you-were-the-director style questions. But they're a really good opportunity to give a good "discussion" — and the more ideas you have, the better.

Section 6 — Types of Question

Appearance & Stage Effects

DIRECTING QUESTIONS

Directors have loads of other stuff to think about as well as how the actors should say their lines.

Mention What Sound and Lighting You'd Use

1) Sound can be used to create a mood. In Act 2, Scene 1, when Richard announces that Clarence is dead, it could change from being quiet and peaceful to having a lot of background noise and exclamations from the other characters. The stage direction, *"They all start"*, suggests this.

2) Lighting is also pretty crucial. There are often clues in the text for what kind of lighting you could use, e.g. In Act 5, Scene 3, Richard says "The sun will not be seen to-day", so the lighting could be fairly dim, to create the impression of an overcast day.

3) Remember to explain every suggestion you make. I know I sound like a broken record saying this, but you absolutely, positively, definitely have to do this. Honestly. I really, really mean it.

Say What Clothes They Should Wear

You can show you understand a scene by talking about the costumes you'd choose for it.

e.g. When Richmond delivers his oration to his soldiers in Act 5, Scene 3, he should be dressed in full armour to show that he is leading his troops into battle, holding his helmet at his side ready for the start of the fight.

You don't have to stick to old-fashioned costumes. Lots of productions today use modern clothes and you can too — as long as you can show how they suit the characters.

Use Loads of Quotes (again)

Just like all the other types of question, you absolutely have to use quotes — but it's actually dead easy to stick a few quotes into these questions. Follow these steps and you're sorted:

- Say how you want the actors to speak and act, and what lighting and sounds you'd use.
- Find a quote that backs your idea up and write it down.
- Say why you'd do it (you won't get the marks otherwise).

Background music? Sound idea...

Just make sure you're still answering the question — if the question just says "What advice would you give to the actors?", don't go on about the lighting or makeup. But if it just says "How would you direct these scenes?", you can talk about pretty much any aspect of the production.

Section 6 — Types of Question

Revision Summary

So there you have it. Four types of exam question, and oodles of tips to help you with each one. Fair enough, some are easier than others — but you've got to be well prepared for any of those types of question, 'cos you just don't know what'll come up in the exam. And if the sight of the very word "exam" has you breaking out in a cold sweat, it's time to really get learning. Right, enough from me, let's have a butcher's at how much attention you've been paying in this section...

1) Give an example of a character who falls in and out of Richard's favour.
2) Which of the following is the best way to work out who all the characters are?
   a) Read the whole play.
   b) Just read the set scenes.
   c) Do loads of historical research.
3) What does "motivation" mean?
4) What does Shakespeare's "use of language" mean?
5) What's another word for "mood"?
6) What should you do if you get a theme question that seems really complicated?
   a) Read the question carefully and work out the main thing it's asking.
   b) Write a good answer on a different subject.
   c) Give up school and become a cattle rancher in Bolivia.
7) True or false? "You don't have to use quotes in theme questions."
8) Name four themes in Richard III that you might be asked about.
9) Explain what is meant by:
   a) anticipation
   b) dramatic irony
10) What does "body language" mean?
11) Give three words or phrases you could use to link different points together.
12) If you talk about clothes, should they always be old-fashioned costumes?
13) What do you absolutely, positively have to do every time you make a point in an essay?
    a) Explain the point and give evidence.
    b) Say what lighting you'd use.
    c) Play a fanfare.

You could cut the tension with a knife.

Section 6 — Types of Question

Section 7 — The Set Scenes

The set scenes are the only scenes you need to know in real detail.
Make sure you know these two scenes inside out.

Act 1 Scene 2
Lines 33 - 186

The bearers take up the coffin

Enter RICHARD.

RICHARD Stay, you that bear the corpse, and set it down.

ANNE What black magician conjures up this fiend
  To stop devoted charitable deeds? 35

RICHARD Villains, set down the corpse or by Saint Paul
  I'll make a corpse of him that disobeys!

GENTLEMAN 1 My lord, stand back and let the coffin pass.

RICHARD Unmannered dog! Stand thou when I command.
  Advance thy halberd higher than my breast — 40
  Or by Saint Paul I'll strike thee to my foot
  And spurn upon thee, beggar, for thy boldness.

The bearers set down the coffin

ANNE What, do you tremble? Are you all afraid?
  Alas, I blame you not, for you are mortal,
  And mortal eyes cannot endure the devil. 45
  Avaunt, thou dreadful minister of hell!
  Thou hadst but power over his mortal body:
  His soul thou canst not have. Therefore be gone!

RICHARD Sweet saint, for charity, be not so curst.

ANNE Foul devil, for God's sake, hence and trouble us not, 50
  For thou hast made the happy earth thy hell,
  Filled it with cursing cries and deep exclaims!
  If thou delight to view thy heinous deeds,
  Behold this pattern of thy butcheries.
  O, gentlemen, see, see! Dead Henry's wounds 55
  Open their congealed mouths and bleed afresh!
  Blush, blush, thou lump of foul deformity,
  For 'tis thy presence that exhales this blood
  From cold and empty veins where no blood dwells.
  Thy deeds inhuman and unnatural 60
  Provokes this deluge most unnatural.
  O God, which this blood mad'st, revenge his death!
  O earth, which this blood drink'st, revenge his death!
  Either heaven with lightning strike the murderer dead;
  Or earth gape open wide and eat him quick — 65
  As thou dost swallow up this good King's blood,
  Which his hell-governed arm hath butcherèd.

RICHARD Lady, you know no rules of charity,
  Which renders good for bad, blessing for curses.

ANNE Villain, thou knowest nor law of God nor man! 70

Anne is mourning for her husband and father-in-law. Richard tries to seduce her by saying her beauty was the reason he killed Henry and Edward.

34-35 'What evil sorcerer has sent you to stop this funeral?'

halberd = combined spear and battleaxe

39-42 'You dog! Stand aside when I tell you to. Stop pointing your halberd at me, or I'll kick you because you're being cheeky.'

43-48 'Are you afraid? I don't blame you — it's natural to be afraid of the devil. Go away, you devil! You only had power over his body — you can't have his soul.'

curst = angry

hence = go away

heinous = horrible

54 'Look at the evidence of your vicious killing.'

55-61 'Look! Henry's wounds are re-opening and bleeding, even though he's dead. You should be ashamed of yourself — they're bleeding because you murdered him.' (In Shakespeare's time some people believed that a victim's wounds would start bleeding again if the murderer was close.)

65-66 The Earth should open up and swallow Richard, just like the ground will absorb Henry's blood.'

68-69 'Lady, you don't understand how to be kind. When a bad thing happens you're supposed to turn it into something positive.'

Section 7 — The Set Scenes

No beast so fierce but knows some touch of pity.
RICHARD But I know none, and therefore am no beast.
ANNE O wonderful, when devils tell the truth!
RICHARD More wonderful when angels are so angry.
    Vouchsafe, divine perfection of a woman, 75
    Of these supposèd crimes to give me leave
    By circumstance but to acquit myself.
ANNE Vouchsafe, diffused infection of a man,
    For these known evils but to give me leave
    By circumstance to curse thy cursèd self. 80
RICHARD Fairer than tongue can name thee, let me have
    Some patient leisure to excuse myself.
ANNE Fouler than heart can think thee, thou canst make
    No excuse current but to hang thyself.
RICHARD By such despair I should accuse myself. 85
ANNE And by despairing shalt thou stand excused
    For doing worthy vengeance on thyself
    That didst unworthy slaughter upon others.
RICHARD Say that I slew them not?
ANNE   Then say they were not slain.
    But dead they are, and, devilish slave, by thee! 90
RICHARD I did not kill your husband.
ANNE   Why, then he is alive.
RICHARD Nay, he is dead, and slain by Edward's hands.
ANNE In thy foul throat thou liest! Queen Margaret saw
    Thy murderous falchion smoking in his blood,
    The which thou once didst bend against her breast, 95
    But that thy brothers beat aside the point.
RICHARD I was provokèd by her slanderous tongue
    That laid their guilt upon my guiltless shoulders.
ANNE Thou wast provokèd by thy bloody mind,
    That never dream'st on aught but butcheries. 100
    Didst thou not kill this King?
RICHARD   I grant ye.
ANNE Dost grant me, hedgehog? Then, God grant me too
    Thou mayst be damnèd for that wicked deed!
    O he was gentle, mild, and virtuous!
RICHARD The better for the King of Heaven, that hath him. 105
ANNE He is in heaven, where thou shalt never come.
RICHARD Let him thank me that holp to send him thither —
    For he was fitter for that place than earth.
ANNE And thou unfit for any place but hell!
RICHARD Yes, one place else, if you will hear me name it. 110
ANNE Some dungeon?

Section 7 — The Set Scenes

RICHARD   Your bed-chamber.
ANNE Ill rest betide the chamber where thou liest!
RICHARD So will it, madam, till I lie with you.
ANNE I hope so!
RICHARD I know so. But, gentle Lady Anne,   115
   To leave this keen encounter of our wits,
   And fall something into a slower method:
   Is not the causer of the timeless deaths
   Of these Plantagenets, Henry and Edward,
   As blameful as the executioner?   120
ANNE Thou wast the cause and most accursed effect.
RICHARD Your beauty was the cause of that effect —
   Your beauty that did haunt me in my sleep
   To undertake the death of all the world
   So I might live one hour in your sweet bosom.   125
ANNE If I thought that, I tell thee, homicide,
   These nails should rend that beauty from my cheeks.
RICHARD These eyes could not endure that beauty's wreck:
   You should not blemish it if I stood by.
   As all the world is cheerèd by the sun,   130
   So I by that; it is my day, my life.
ANNE Black night o'ershade thy day, and death thy life.
RICHARD Curse not thyself, fair creature — thou art both.
ANNE I would I were, to be revenged on thee.
RICHARD It is a quarrel most unnatural,   135
   To be revenged on him that loveth thee.
ANNE It is a quarrel just and reasonable,
   To be revenged on him that killed my husband.
RICHARD He that bereft thee, lady, of thy husband
   Did it to help thee to a better husband.   140
ANNE His better doth not breathe upon the earth.
RICHARD He lives that loves thee better than he could.
ANNE Name him.
RICHARD   Plantagenet.
ANNE   Why that was he.
RICHARD The self-same name, but one of better nature.
ANNE Where is he?
RICHARD   Here. *(She spits at him)* Why dost thou
              spit at me? 145
ANNE Would it were mortal poison, for thy sake!
RICHARD Never came poison from so sweet a place.
ANNE Never hung poison on a fouler toad.
   Out of my sight! Thou dost infect mine eyes.

---

betide = happen to

112 'I hope you don't get any sleep in your bedroom.'

115-120 'Lady Anne, let's stop arguing and talk this through. Isn't the person that caused me to kill Henry and Edward as much to blame as I am.'

Plantagenet = the surname of the royal family

122-125 'Your beauty caused me to kill Henry and Edward. I thought that if I killed Henry I would be able to be with you.'

126-127 'If that's true, I'd rather scratch my face off than be with you.'

128-131 'I couldn't cope with seeing the loss of your beauty. I wouldn't allow it to happen. Like the world is brightened by the sun, your beauty brightens my day and my life.'

132 'I hope your day becomes your night and you die.'

133 'By saying that, you curse yourself because you're my life.'

bereft = deprived

141 'There is no one alive better than my husband.'

143 'My husband had that name.'

146 'I wish my spit was poisonous.'

Section 7 — The Set Scenes

150 *'Your eyes have a powerful effect on me.'*

basilisks = deadly mythical reptiles

152-171 *'Your harsh look kills me, you have made me cry because you're so beautiful. I've never cried before, not even when the Earl of Rutland was killed by Clifford, or when your father told me that my father had died. I've never said anything romantic before either, but your beauty has changed that as well.'*

175-179 *'Here's my sword. If you want you can kill me and let my adoring soul go free. I won't defend myself — I beg for you to kill me.'*

184 *'Pick up the sword again, or agree to be with me.'*

dissembler = deceiver

RICHARD Thine eyes, sweet lady, have infected mine.   150
ANNE Would they were basilisks to strike thee dead!
RICHARD I would they were, that I might die at once;
  For now they kill me with a living death.
  Those eyes of thine from mine have drawn salt tears,
  Shamed their aspects with store of childish drops;   155
  These eyes, which never shed remorseful tear,
  No, when my father York and Edward wept
  To hear the piteous moan that Rutland made
  When black-faced Clifford shook his sword at him;
  Nor when thy warlike father, like a child,   160
  Told the sad story of my father's death,
  And twenty times made pause to sob and weep
  That all the standers-by had wet their cheeks
  Like trees bedashed with rain. In that sad time
  My manly eyes did scorn an humble tear;   165
  And what these sorrows could not thence exhale
  Thy beauty hath, and made them blind with weeping.
  I never sued to friend nor enemy;
  My tongue could never learn sweet smoothing word.
  But, now thy beauty is proposed my fee,   170
  My proud heart sues, and prompts my tongue to speak.

She looks scornfully at him.

RICHARD Teach not thy lip such scorn for it was made
  For kissing, lady, not for such contempt.
  If thy revengeful heart cannot forgive,
  Lo here I lend thee this sharp-pointed sword,   175
  Which if thou please to hide in this true breast
  And let the soul forth that adoreth thee,
  I lay it naked to the deadly stroke,
  And humbly beg the death upon my knee.

Kneeling he opens his shirt. She grips the sword and moves towards him as if to stab him.

  Nay, do not pause: for I did kill King Henry —   180
  But 'twas thy beauty that provokèd me.
  Nay, now dispatch: 'twas I that stabbed young Edward —
  But 'twas thy heavenly face that set me on.

She drops the sword.

  Take up the sword again, or take up me.
ANNE Arise, dissembler. Though I wish thy death,   185
  I will not be thy executioner.

Section 7 — The Set Scenes

Act 4 Scene 4
Lines 199 - 342

> Richard tries to persuade Queen Elizabeth to let him marry her daughter, Elizabeth. The Queen disagrees and they argue.

KING RICHARD Stay, madam. I must talk a word with you.
ELIZABETH I have no more sons of the royal blood   200
    For thee to slaughter! For my daughters, Richard,
    They shall be praying nuns, not weeping queens —
    And therefore level not to hit their lives.

203 'Don't set out to punish them.'

level = aim

KING RICHARD You have a daughter called Elizabeth,
    Virtuous and fair, royal and gracious.   205
ELIZABETH And must she die for this? O, let her live,
    And I'll corrupt her manners, stain her beauty,
    Slander myself as false to Edward's bed,
    Throw over her the veil of infamy!
    So she may live unscarred of bleeding slaughter,   210
    I will confess she was not Edward's daughter.

208-211 'I'll lie and say Elizabeth is illegitimate, then she'll be no use to you and she'll be protected from your violent nature.'

KING RICHARD Wrong not her birth. She is a royal Princess.
ELIZABETH To save her life I'll say she is not so.
KING RICHARD Her life is safest only in her birth.
ELIZABETH And only in that safety died her brothers.   215
KING RICHARD Lo, at their birth good stars were opposite.
ELIZABETH No, to their lives ill friends were contrary.
KING RICHARD All unavoided is the doom of destiny.
ELIZABETH True, when avoided grace makes destiny.
    My babes were destined to a fairer death,   220
    If grace had blessed *thee* with a fairer life.
KING RICHARD You speak as if that I had slain my cousins.
ELIZABETH Cousins, indeed! And by their uncle cozened
    Of comfort, kingdom, kindred, freedom, life!
    Whose hand soever lanced their tender hearts,   225
    Thy head, all indirectly, gave direction.
    No doubt the murderous knife was dull and blunt
    Till it was whetted on thy stone-hard heart
    To revel in the entrails of my lambs!
    But that still use of grief makes wild grief tame,   230
    My tongue should to thy ears not name my boys
    Till that my nails were anchored in thine eyes —
    And I, in such a desperate bay of death,
    Like a poor bark, of sails and tackling reft,
    Rush all to pieces on thy rocky bosom.   235

216 'They were born under unlucky stars, which means their lives are cursed.'

217 'No, it's bad friends that have caused them to have bad luck.'

218 'Their cursed destiny was unavoidable.'

219-221 'That's true, when a person without kindness (Richard) controls my children's destiny. My children would have had a fairer death if you had been a better person.'

cozened = cheated

lanced = stabbed

225-235 'Whoever killed them, it was you who gave the order. I bet the knife used to murder them was blunt until it was sharpened by your cold heart so it could enjoy my children's guts. Talking about this calms me down so I shouldn't say more until I'm clawing your eyes out. I feel like I'm a helpless ship in a bay and you're the rock that I'm going to crash into.'

KING RICHARD Madam, so thrive I in my enterprise
    And dangerous success of bloody wars,
    As I intend more good to you or yours
    Than ever you or yours by me were harmed!

236-239 'Madam, I'm happy that I've succeeded in my bloodthirsty schemes because I'm going to do a good deed for you which will make up for all the bad things I've done.'

Section 7 — The Set Scenes

54

240-241 'What could possibly do me any good now?

scaffold = where people were executed

demise = give

249-254 'I'll give everything I have to a child of yours, so you'll forget every bad deed you think I've committed against you.'

Lethe = river in Greek mythology that caused forgetfulness

254-255 'Get to the point, or you'll spend longer talking about it than doing anything about it.'

259 'Your love for my daughter is separate from your soul.'

confound = confuse

266 'Me, of course.'

humour = personality

274 Queen Margaret and her husband, Henry VI, were enemies of Richard's family.

ELIZABETH What good is covered with the face of heaven, 240
  To be discovered, that can do me good?
KING RICHARD Th' advancement of your children, gentle lady.
ELIZABETH Up to some scaffold, there to lose their heads?
KING RICHARD Unto the dignity and height of fortune,
  The high imperial type of this earth's glory! 245
ELIZABETH Flatter my sorrow with report of it.
  Tell me what state, what dignity, what honour,
  Canst thou demise to any child of mine?
KING RICHARD Even all I have — ay, and myself and all
  Will I withal endow a child of thine — 250
  So in the Lethe of thy angry soul
  Thou drown the sad remembrance of those wrongs
  Which thou supposest I have done to thee.
ELIZABETH Be brief, lest that the process of thy kindness
  Last longer telling than thy kindness' date. 255
KING RICHARD Then know, that from my soul I love thy daughter.
ELIZABETH My daughter's mother thinks it with her soul.
KING RICHARD What do you think?
ELIZABETH That thou dost love my daughter "from" thy soul.
  So from thy soul's love didst thou love her brothers, 260
  And from my heart's love I do thank thee for it!
KING RICHARD Be not so hasty to confound my meaning.
  I mean that with my soul I love thy daughter
  And do intend to make her Queen of England.
ELIZABETH Well, then, who dost thou mean shall be her king? 265
KING RICHARD Even he that makes her Queen. Who else
  should be?
ELIZABETH What, *thou*?
KING RICHARD   Even so. How think you of it?
ELIZABETH How canst *thou* woo her?
KING RICHARD   That would I learn of you,
  As one being best acquainted with her humour.
ELIZABETH And wilt thou learn of me?
KING RICHARD   Madam, with all my heart. 270
ELIZABETH Send to her, by the man that slew her brothers,
  A pair of bleeding hearts. Thereon engrave
  "Edward" and "York". Then haply will she weep.
  Therefore present to her — as sometime Margaret
  Did to thy father, steeped in Rutland's blood — 275

Section 7 — The Set Scenes

A handkerchief: which, say to her, did drain
The purple sap from her sweet brother's body,
And bid her wipe her weeping eyes withal.
If this inducement move her not to love,
Send her a letter of thy noble deeds. 280
Tell her thou mad'st away her uncle Clarence,
Her uncle Rivers — ay, and for her sake
Mad'st quick conveyance with her good aunt Anne.

KING RICHARD You mock me, madam. This is not the way
To win your daughter.

ELIZABETH   There is no other way — 285
Unless thou couldst put on some other shape
And not be Richard that hath done all this!

KING RICHARD Say that I did all this for love of her.

ELIZABETH Nay, then indeed she cannot choose but hate thee,
Having bought love with such a bloody spoil! 290

KING RICHARD Look what is done cannot be now amended!
Men shall deal unadvisedly sometimes,
Which after-hours gives leisure to repent.
If I did take the kingdom from your sons,
To make amends I'll give it to your daughter. 295
If I have killed the issue of your womb,
To quicken your increase I will beget
Mine issue of your blood upon your daughter.
A grandam's name is little less in love
Than is the doting title of a mother. 300
They are as children but one step below,
Even of your metal, of your very blood —
Of all one pain, save for a night of groans
Endured of her, for whom you bid like sorrow.
Your children were vexation to your youth; 305
But mine shall be a comfort to your age.
The loss you have is but a son being King,
And by that loss your daughter is made Queen.
I cannot make you what amends I would,
Therefore accept such kindness as I can. 310
Dorset your son, that with a fearful soul
Leads discontented steps in foreign soil,
This fair alliance quickly shall call home
To high promotions and great dignity.
The King, that calls your beauteous daughter wife, 315
Familiarly shall call thy Dorset brother.
Again shall you be mother to a king,
And all the ruins of distressful times
Repaired with double riches of content.

276-279 'Give her a hanky and tell her it mopped up her brother's blood, then tell her to dry her eyes with it.'

inducement = persuasion

281-283 'Tell her you killed Clarence, Uncle Rivers and Anne as well.'

285-287 'There's no way you can get my daughter Elizabeth, unless you become someone else.'

291-298 'I can't change what happened. Sometimes people make mistakes. If I did take the kingdom from your sons, to make up for it I'll give it to your daughter. I'll also give you another child with Elizabeth.'

beget = give rise to

grandam's = grandmother's

301-306 'Your daughter's children are connected to you by blood and also by the pain of childbirth. Your children annoyed you when you were young, but mine will comfort you in your old age.'

311-319 'Your son Dorset (who is unhappy in a foreign country at the moment) will come home to see the marriage of his sister. He'll be promoted here to a better position. This marriage will bring the family closer together.'

Section 7 — The Set Scenes

320-324 *'The future is bright, the tears you have cried will turn into riches and you will be very happy.'*

wooer = seducer

328-330 *'Go and talk to her, and prepare her for my attempts to seduce her. Put the idea in her head that she could be Queen and tell her how wonderful marriage is.'*

chastised = disciplined

336 *'She'll be victorious like Caesar.'*

337-342 *'What should I say? Her father's brother is going to marry her? Or should I call you her uncle? How should I make her agree to something that's against God, the law, my honour and her love?'*

> What! We have many goodly days to see!   320
> The liquid drops of tears that you have shed
> Shall come again, transformed to orient pearl,
> Advantaging their loan with interest
> Of ten times double gain of happiness!
> Go then, my mother — to thy daughter go.   325
> Make bold her bashful years with your experience.
> Prepare her ears to hear a wooer's tale.
> Put in her tender heart th' aspiring flame
> Of golden sovereignty! Acquaint the Princess
> With the sweet silent hours of marriage joys.   330
> And when this arm of mine hath chastisèd
> The petty rebel, dull-brained Buckingham,
> Bound with triumphant garlands will I come,
> And lead thy daughter to a conqueror's bed —
> To whom I will retail my conquest won,   335
> And she shall be sole victoress, Caesar's Caesar!
> ELIZABETH What were I best to say? Her father's brother
> Would be her lord? Or shall I say her uncle?
> Or he that slew her brothers and her uncles?
> Under what title shall I woo for thee   340
> That God, the law, my honour, and her love
> Can make seem pleasing to her tender years?

Section 7 — The Set Scenes

Index

A
acts 3
adjectives 2
Anne 21, 26, 38
anticipation 45
appearance 47
Archbishop of York 16, 23
argument 33
aside 4
asterisk * 36
atmosphere 41
audience 4

B
Battle of Bosworth 15, 28, 29
beginning, middle and end 33
Bishop of Ely 16, 25
Blunt 14, 28
body language 46
bottled spider 12
Brakenbury 9, 14, 26
Buckingham 9, 14, 20, 23-28, 38, 39

C
Cardinal Bourchier 24
Catesby 9, 14, 25-27, 29
character questions 38, 39
checking for mistakes 36
citizens 16, 23, 25
Clarence 9, 13, 19-23
clothes 47
conclusion 36
conscience 20
coronation 25
corrections 36
crimes 20
curses 12, 19, 24

D
Dighton 16, 20
directing questions 44-47
Dorset 9, 13, 23, 26
dramatic irony 24, 45
dreams 19, 20
dropping letters 6
Duchess of York 9, 12, 23, 26, 27
Duke of Gloucester 9
Duke of York 9, 11, 23, 24, 26

E
Earl of Derby 15
Edward IV 9, 11, 20, 23
Elizabeth 26
essay 31, 33
exam 1, 31
examples 2, 31
exeunt 3
explanation 32, 46, 47
extra letters 6

F
fate 19
Forrest 16, 20

G
ghosts 15, 28
good and evil 20
grammar 36
Grey 9, 13, 23, 24
guilt 20

H
Hastings 9, 14, 21, 23-25, 38
Henry VI 18, 19, 21
Herbert 14
history 4, 18
House of Lancaster 18, 21, 29
House of York 18, 21, 29

I
interesting words 35
introductions 35

K
Keeper of the Tower 16
key points 36

L
Lady Anne 9, 12
language questions 40, 41
lighting 47
line numbers 3, 32
linking words 46
Lord Cardinal 16
Lord Mayor 16, 25
Lovell 14, 25

Index

lying 40

M
mistakes 36
mood 32, 41, 46
motivation 39
murderers 16, 19, 20, 22

N
Nobles 14

O
old language 5, 6
opening paragraphs 35
oration 28

P
paragraphs 2, 32
planning 1, 31, 33, 34
poetry 7
preparation 1
Prince Edward 9, 11, 23-26, 40
prose 7
punctuation 2, 5, 36
Pursuivant 16

Q
Queen Elizabeth 9, 11, 22, 23, 27
Queen Margaret 9, 12, 18, 19, 22, 27, 40
quotations 2, 32-34, 41, 42, 47

R
Ratcliffe 9, 14, 24, 25, 27, 28
remorse 20
rewards 10
rhyming couplets 7
Richard 9, 10, 19-23, 25, 27, 29, 38-40
Richmond 9, 15, 28, 29
Rivers 9, 13, 23, 24
royal family 4

S
sanctuary 11, 23, 24, 26
sarcasm 40
scenes 3
Scrivener 16, 25
set scenes 1, 33, 49-56

Sheriff 16
Sir Christopher Urswick 16, 27
Sir Thomas Vaughan 13
soliloquy 4
sounds 47
speech marks 2
spelling 2, 36
stage directions 3, 44
Stanley 9, 15, 19, 24-28
Stanley's son 27, 28
strawberries 16
structure 33, 34
style 35
summing up 36
suspense 45
syllables 7

T
theme questions 42, 43
thou, thee and thy 6
tone of voice 45, 46
Tower 21, 24, 26
Tudor Myth 18
Tyrrel 9, 16, 26

U
ugliness 10
underlining 31, 34

V
Vaughan 23, 24
verbs 6
versions of the play 2, 4

W
Wars of the Roses 18
who's in favour 38
Woodvilles 9, 13, 23, 24
word order 5

Y
young princes 9, 11, 18, 23, 24, 26